Andrew S

# WINTERLONG

## NICK HERN BOOKS

London

www.nickhernbooks.co.uk

**A Nick Hern Book**

*Winterlong* first published in Great Britain in 2011 as a paperback original by Nick Hern Books Limited, 14 Larden Road, London W3 7ST

*Winterlong* copyright © 2011 Andrew Sheridan

Andrew Sheridan has asserted his right to be identified as the author of this work

Cover image: Hip Replacement
Cover design: Ned Hoste

Typeset by Nick Hern Books
Printed and bound in Great Britain by CLE Print Ltd, St Ives, Cambs, PE27 3LE

A CIP catalogue record for this book is available from the British Library

ISBN 978 1 84842 130 1

**CAUTION** All rights whatsoever in this translation are strictly reserved. Requests to reproduce the text in whole or in part should be addressed to the publisher.

**Amateur Performing Rights** Applications for performance, including readings and excerpts, by amateurs in English should be addressed to the Performing Rights Manager, Nick Hern Books, 14 Larden Road, London W3 7ST, *tel* +44 (0)20 8749 4953, *fax* +44 (0)20 8735 0250, *e-mail* info@nickhernbooks.demon.co.uk, except as follows:

*Australia*: Dominie Drama, 8 Cross Street, Brookvale 2100, *fax* (2) 9938 8695, *e-mail* drama@dominie.com.au

*New Zealand*: Play Bureau, PO Box 420, New Plymouth, *fax* (6) 753 2150, *e-mail* play.bureau.nz@xtra.co.nz

*South Africa*: DALRO (pty) Ltd, PO Box 31627, 2017 Braamfontein, *tel* (11) 712 8000, *fax* (11) 403 9094, *e-mail* theatricals@dalro.co.za

*United States of America and Canada*: Casarotto Ramsay and Associates Ltd, see details below

**Professional Performing Rights** Applications for performance by professionals in any medium and in any language throughout the world (and amateur and stock performances in the United States of America and Canada) should be addressed to Casarotto Ramsay and Associates Ltd, Waverley House, 7–12 Noel Street, London W1F 8GQ, *fax* +44 (0)20 7287 9128, *e-mail* agents@casarotto.co.uk

No performance of any kind may be given unless a licence has been obtained. Applications should be made before rehearsals begin. Publication of this play does not necessarily indicate its availability for amateur performance.

**FSC**
The mark of responsible forestry
TT-COC-003115
FSC Trademark © 1996 Forest Stewardship Council A.C

*Winterlong* was first performed at the Royal Exchange Theatre, Manchester, on 2 February 2011, with the following cast:

| | |
|---|---|
| OSCAR/BOY | Harry McEntire |
| HELEN/GIRL | Rebecca Callard |
| JOHN | Paul Copley |
| MALCOLM/NEIL/PHILIP | Laurence Mitchell |
| JEAN | Gabrielle Reidy |

| | |
|---|---|
| *Director* | Sarah Frankcom |
| *Designer* | Amanda Stoodley |
| *Lighting Designer* | Richard Owen |
| *Sound Designer* | Peter Rice |
| *Dialect Coach* | Joe Windley |
| *Assistant Director* | Andy Rogers |

| | |
|---|---|
| *Producer* | Richard Morgan |
| *Production Manager* | Keith Broom |
| *Stage Manager* | Julia Wade |
| *Deputy Stage Manager* | Tracey Fleet |
| *Props and Setting Supervisors* | Andy Bubble, Phil Costello |
| *With help from* | Ben Cook, Simon Pemberton, Will Gaskell |
| *Wardrobe Supervisor* | Felicia Jagne |

*Set and props by the Royal Exchange Theatre Company props and setting department*

*Costumes by the Royal Exchange Theatre Company wardrobe department*

The production transferred to Soho Theatre, London, on 23 February 2011.

# the bruntwood prize for playwriting

## in partnership with the
## Royal Exchange Theatre

WINTERLONG was one of the joint winners of the Bruntwood Prize in 2008. The biggest national competition of its kind, the Bruntwood is the search for great new plays and great writers. Its awards support writers and help them develop their work with a view to production.

To find out more about the Prize and how to enter visit writeaplay.co.uk

# WINTERLONG

Andrew Sheridan

*For Rebecca*

**Author's Note**

I would like to thank Sarah Frankcom, everyone at the Royal Exchange, as well as Mike Oglesby and Bruntwood.

I would also like to offer heartfelt thanks to Robert Holman, David Eldridge and Simon Stephens, who I will be forever indebted to for their support, belief and inspiration. Three great men. Three great friends.

## Characters

BOY, *eight*
HELEN, *fifteen to twenty-six*
JOHN, *fifty-five to sixty-seven*
MALCOLM
JEAN, *fifty-six to sixty-five*
NEIL
OSCAR, *six (offstage) to fifteen*
PHILIP
GIRL, *fifteen*

## Setting and Time

The play takes place in and around Manchester, though this isn't strictly important. The action spans fifteen years of Oscar's life. It could take place anywhere and in any time.

The set should be non-naturalistic and should be evoked by space, detail, lighting and sound rather than realism.

Some characters could be played by the same actor with the exception of John, Jean, and Oscar.

Punctuation is used to indicate delivery, not to conform to the rules of grammar.

*This text went to press before the end of rehearsals and so may differ slightly from the play as performed.*

## Scene One

*Bonfire Night. A wall by a canal. A broken street lamp.*

*It is nearly dark.*

*The odd firework explodes.*

*Bonfire mist and the smell of sulphur.*

*The sound of a fire engine in the distance.*

*Moonlight falls on the hard outline of a pregnant schoolgirl sat on the wall.*

*It is* HELEN *(fifteen). She has two cut knees.*

*A plastic carrier bag of shopping lies at her feet.*

*She strikes a match on the wall.*

*She lights a cigarette and her face is brightened by the flame.*

*She lets the whole match burn.*

*She throws it in the canal.*

*She smokes the cigarette.*

*She rubs her stomach.*

*The street lamp starts to buzz and flicker. It casts intermittent orange light over the canal and falls on the shape of a* BOY *standing underneath.*

*He is silent and still.*

*He watches* HELEN.

*She doesn't see him.*

HELEN *(singing)*. Two dead dogs sitting on a wall,
    Two dead dogs sitting on a wall,
    And if one dead dog should accidentally fall,
    There'll be one dead dog sitting on a wall.

*The street lamp settles.*

*The* BOY *is soaking wet and wearing white underpants and vest.*

*He holds a pair of red wellington boots in his hands.*

HELEN *becomes aware of his presence. She hardens. She doesn't look at him.*

BOY. You shouldn't smoke. Give your baby cancer. Make it all small and poisoned. Might come out with no head. Might come out with no head no arms no legs. Just a body. Not even nipples. Not even a belly button. Just a pale body like a bag of milk.

*He turns the two wellington boots upside down and water pours from them onto the floor. It forms a puddle at his feet.*

*The* BOY *puts the wellington boots on.*

*He kicks and stamps the puddle.*

Give us a bit of that cig.

HELEN. Too young to smoke.

BOY. You better give us some.

HELEN. Or what?

BOY. Or I'll come over there and punch that rat in your fat ugly stomach so hard it comes out of your mouth and dies in the dirt. That's what.

*Pause.*

I'll do it. I touched a tramp's hand this morning. She had shit under her fingernails and I still did it. If I can do that I can do anything.

HELEN. Told you.

BOY. Fuck off you slag.

*The* BOY *picks up a stone from the floor and throws it at* HELEN.

I said fuck off you slag you deaf cunt.

HELEN *spits at the* BOY.

(*Wounded and wiping the spit off himself.*) Fuck off. Mong head.

HELEN. Why do you swear so much?

*The* BOY *gives her the finger and mouths 'fuck off' silently.*

*He looks at the floor.*

*Pause.*

BOY. I saw three dead cats in there today. They just floated past my face when I was swimming. People fling them in there all the time. They just melt and fall to bits. I'd kill all the cats in the world if it was up to me. That's what I'd do if I was fucking God.

*Pause.*

Please can I have a bit?

HELEN. Give you cancer.

BOY. I'm not scared.

HELEN. You will be when your balls drop off.

BOY. I won't be. I don't believe in cancer. I don't believe in anything me. I want to see the whole world burn down.

*Screaming fireworks explode and wail.*

HELEN *goes to leave.*

(*Stopping her.*) It's my birthday. That's what it is. Today.

*The* BOY *sits on the wall.*

HELEN *stops.*

*She returns to the wall and gives the* BOY *the cigarette.*

HELEN. Happy birthday.

*The* BOY *goes to smoke the cigarette but stamps on it instead.*

BOY. Shouldn't fucking smoke.

HELEN *slaps the* BOY *hard across the face.*

*The* BOY *tries to shield himself.*

*As the attack escalates the smacks become full-on punches. It is brutal and ugly and painful.*

HELEN (*smacking*). You.

(*Smacking.*) Stink.

(*Smacking.*) Of.

(*Smacking.*) Dog.

(*Smacking.*) Shit.

(*Punching.*) You.

(*Punching.*) Skinny.

(*Punching.*) Fucking.

(*Punching.*) Pig.

(*Punching.*) Baby.

What you crying for?

Why you crying?

That was my last one.

Stop it.

*Pause.*

I hate people crying.

HELEN *gets a loaf of bread and a jar of jam from the carrier bag on the floor.*

*She takes a slice of bread and puts it on her knee.*

*She opens the jam jar and dips her fingers into it and scoops out some jam.*

*She puts the jam on the slice of bread and folds it in half.*

*She offers the jam sandwich to the* BOY.

Here.

*The* BOY *wipes his nose on his knee and takes the sandwich.*

*He begins to eat it a corner at a time.*

HELEN *puts her fingers in her mouth and sucks the jam off them.*

*She puts the lid on the jam jar and puts it and the loaf of bread back into the carrier bag.*

HELEN *looks at her reflection in the canal.*

*It begins to snow.*

BOY. See that bike? I'd never throw it in there if it was mine. I'd polish it every day. Been trying to get it out for weeks. Keep running out of breath. Wish I was a fish sometimes. I could stay down there for ever then.

*The* BOY *shivers.*

HELEN. It's too cold to be swimming in the canal. You'll die you you know. I've seen it happen loads of times. When you're under the water it'll freeze over and you'll be trapped in there for ever. They'll find you in hundreds of years. Defrost you and put you in a museum in a glass case. All brown and shrivelled with a giant head.

HELEN *takes her coat off.*

You should put my coat on.

BOY. I don't feel the cold me.

*The* BOY *shivers.*

HELEN *throws the coat toward the* BOY.

*It lands on the floor between them.*

*The* BOY *hesitates before putting the coat on.*

I'm only putting it on because you want me to.

*The* BOY *shivers.*

How did you do that? Your knee?

*Beat.*

HELEN. Don't know.

*The* BOY *puts his hand in the canal.*

*He cleans* HELEN*'s knee with the water.*

*He takes one plaster from his own knee and puts it on* HELEN*'s cut knee.*

HELEN *rubs her pregnant stomach.*

*The* BOY *watches.*

BOY. Can I have a go?

*Beat.*

HELEN. Dry your hands off.

*The* BOY *dries his hands.*

Warm your hands up then. Rub them together.

*The* BOY *rubs his hands together.*

HELEN *takes his hand and puts it on her stomach.*

Can you feel its foot sticking out?

BOY. Yes.

HELEN. When I'm in the bath you can see it sometimes. Sticking right out. Like a doll inside a balloon.

BOY. Can I listen?

HELEN *hesitates but lets the* BOY *put his ear to her stomach.*

HELEN *puts her hand on the* BOY*'s head and strokes his hair.*

I wish I was him inside your stomach. I don't think I'd ever come out. I think I'd stay in there for ever. Hanging on to your insides. You're going to be the best mum in the world. I think that you should know that.

*A firework explodes overhead, showering them both with an incredible illumination that hangs above them as the moment freezes in time.*

*They both look at each other and don't look away.*

You could call him Oscar. That's my name. I think he'd like it.

HELEN. Might not be an him.

BOY. It is.

HELEN. How do you know?

BOY. I know everything me.

HELEN. Can I have my coat back? I'm going to miss my bus. My mum will kill me if I lose that one. Lost about three already. Not even Christmas yet. Always losing everything me.

*The* BOY *takes the coat off and offers it back to* HELEN.

*She puts it on.*

BOY (*singing*). One dead dog sitting on the wall,
    One dead dog sitting on the wall,
    And if that dead dog should accidentally fall,
    There'll be no dead dog sitting on the wall.

HELEN (*as he sings*). I hope my baby's just like you. I think I could love him for ever. I'd hold his hand and never let him go.

*Another firework explodes with a deafening bang and a blinding flash.*

*Darkness.*

*The* BOY *disappears.*

*Moonlight.*

HELEN*'s waters have broken. It steams as it hits the floor.*

HELEN *is left in the moonlight giving birth to her son,* OSCAR.

## Scene Two

*Two years later. February. A secluded part of a bus station.*

*It is three o'clock in the morning.*

*Darkness gives way to oppressive fluorescent lighting.*

*The sound of plastic seats flapping in the wind.*

*Hard rain batters the metal roof.*

*The rain drips and collects in small puddles on the floor.*

*Somewhere in a different part of the station, a woman howls. It echoes through the space and dies suddenly.*

JOHN *(fifty-five) is perched on a tall plastic waiting seat. Next to him is* OSCAR *(two) in a pram.*

*He takes out a flask and pours himself a cup of coffee.*

*He sips it.*

MALCOLM *enters carrying a cardboard box.*

*He is dressed in a black suit. The trousers of which are hitched up with bicycle clips.*

*He doesn't have a bike.*

MALCOLM. I've been to a funeral.

*Pause.*

I said I've been to a funeral.

*Pause.*

That's where I've been. To a funeral. It's been a particularly difficult day. You know. Emotionally.

*Pause.*

Life. It can be such an anti-climax don't you think? I say
funeral. It was a cremation.

*Pause.*

I don't suppose you would be interested in sharing that flask?
I wouldn't normally be so forward. I wouldn't normally
request the company of a stranger. But I've had somewhat of
a lonely day and beggars can't be choosers. Not thirty-seven
minutes past three and eighteen seconds in the morning. I'm
not a scrounger. I've got some Bourbon Creams. We could
do a swap.

JOHN *pours* MALCOLM *a cup of coffee from the flask.*

*He offers* MALCOLM *the cup.*

MALCOLM *takes a packet of Bourbon Creams from his
coat pocket.*

MALCOLM *offers them to* JOHN.

*They both exchange their offerings.*

I always carry a fresh packet of biscuits and a clean
handkerchief. You never know when they might come in
handy.

MALCOLM *whistles a long continuous note until his breath
runs out.*

I hope you don't mind me admitting that asking you to share
your coffee is the bravest act of connection I've ever
attempted in my life.

JOHN *smiles.*

MALCOLM *dunks a Bourbon Cream into his coffee and
eats it.*

My name is Malcolm by the way.

JOHN *nods.*

Do you mind me asking who's in the pram?

*Pause.*

The pram. Who's in the pram?

JOHN *looks at* MALCOLM.

Sorry. I've overstepped the mark haven't I? I should learn to walk before I can run.

JOHN. He has trouble sleeping.

MALCOLM. Really?

JOHN. So do I.

MALCOLM. Really?

JOHN. A walk in the night seems to help.

MALCOLM. Yes.

What's he called?

JOHN *is silent*.

I've had two teeth out. Two molars.

MALCOLM *shows* JOHN.

JOHN *doesn't really want to see*.

JOHN. Yes.

MALCOLM. My gums were bleeding for hours. I had to put toilet paper in the holes where my teeth had been.

MALCOLM *shows* JOHN.

JOHN *doesn't want to see*.

JOHN. It's my grandson. Oscar.

MALCOLM. Oscar. I don't think I've ever met an Oscar. I collect names.

*Beat*.

Do you think I could sneak a peek?

JOHN *nods*.

MALCOLM *goes over to the pram and looks in*.

He's tiny. Still looks like a proper baby.

JOHN. He's two.

*Beat.*

He's not disabled.

MALCOLM. That's good.

*Pause.*

He has a very distinct odour. I have a very astute sense of smell. Always have done. I can smell a fox a mile off. It's a talent I inherited from my mother.

*Pause.*

He looks like you. Same ears. He must make you feel very happy. Fulfilled even.

JOHN. He does. I am.

MALCOLM. I'd like to be a granddad one day. I'd have to be a father first I suppose. I'm not really a woman sort of man though.

*Beat.*

JOHN. You might struggle then.

*Beat.*

MALCOLM. Yes. I might. I suppose.

JOHN *stands up and prepares to leave.*

Robert was attacked by a stray cocker spaniel this morning. The dog didn't cause any physical damage but Robert's very sensitive. I think it's more of a psychological injury. They often take longer to heal. It will probably take him a while to gather enough confidence before he feels comfortable to be out in public on his own again. It's a shame. He's always been such a free spirit. I feel very responsible. If we hadn't of argued. If I hadn't of lost my temper and locked him out of the house then none of this might have happened. Who would have thought a ham salad could cause such anguish.

JOHN. Who's Robert?

MALCOLM. Robert. My pet tortoise.

JOHN. Right.

MALCOLM. He's in that box. I had to take him to the funeral
with me. Sat him on a prayer cushion. I tried to find a black
box as a mark of respect but they're very hard to come by.

JOHN *drains his cup quickly and puts the flask away.*

What's your name?

JOHN. I don't think I want to tell you my name.

MALCOLM. I'd like to know your name. Like I said I collect
them. Store them up here.

JOHN *studies* MALCOLM.

Okay. Well, see you then. Thank you for the cup.

JOHN. Yes.

MALCOLM. Night.

JOHN. Goodnight.

*Beat.*

I hope your tortoise gets better.

MALCOLM. So do I.

JOHN *goes to leave.*

MALCOLM *suddenly sings the theme tune to* Jim'll Fix It.

JOHN *stops.*

*He watches him.*

JOHN (*as* MALCOLM *sings*). You're singing.

*Pause.*

Are you singing?

*Pause.*

Stop singing.

MALCOLM *finishes the theme tune to* Jim'll Fix It.

Right then.

MALCOLM (*the bravest thing he has ever asked in his life*). I haven't quite figured out how all this works. The mechanics of the situation.

*Beat.*

I give up. (*Holding his hands up.*) I surrender.

*Beat.*

I think I would like to have sex with you.

JOHN *is silent.*

Has that come as a shock to you?

JOHN. It has a little.

MALCOLM. You look petrified.

JOHN. I am. A little.

MALCOLM. Are you?

JOHN. Yes. I am.

MALCOLM. Don't be.

JOHN. Right.

MALCOLM. There's no need.

JOHN. Isn't there?

MALCOLM. No. There's absolutely no point in being the slightest bit afraid of what I'm going to do to you.

JOHN. Right.

MALCOLM. I'm going to undo my belt.

MALCOLM *undoes his belt.*

I'm going to unzip my flies.

MALCOLM *opens his flies.*

I'm taking my trousers down.

JOHN. I don't think this is right.

MALCOLM. Unfortunately you don't have a choice in the matter any longer.

*MALCOLM drops his trousers down to his ankles.*

*MALCOLM shuffles towards JOHN.*

*MALCOLM stands face to face with JOHN.*

*It's as if they might kiss.*

*MALCOLM gently strokes JOHN's face.*

JOHN. I think I should get home.

*Beat.*

I think this is a mistake.

*Beat.*

I've got money. I've got fifteen pound. You can have it.

*Beat.*

We can just pretend nothing has happened.

MALCOLM. We can't.

JOHN. I could just go.

MALCOLM. You can't.

JOHN. Please don't.

*MALCOLM pulls his trousers up.*

I'm going. Thank you.

*MALCOLM slaps JOHN across the face.*

MALCOLM. Do you drink pints of cum?

JOHN. No.

*MALCOLM slaps JOHN across the face.*

MALCOLM. I bet you wanted to drink a pint of mine.

JOHN. I didn't.

MALCOLM *slaps* JOHN *across the face*.

MALCOLM. Are you lying?

JOHN. No.

MALCOLM. Take your trousers down.

JOHN *unzips his trousers*.

You've fucked men ant you?

JOHN. No.

MALCOLM *rips* JOHN*'s trousers down*.

MALCOLM. Did you cum?

JOHN. I haven't…

JOHN *is now stood with his trousers round his ankles exposing his underwear*.

MALCOLM. Did you orgasm?

JOHN *shivers*.

Did they wank in your face?

JOHN. No.

MALCOLM. Did they cum in your mouth?

JOHN. No.

MALCOLM. Did you cum in their mouth?

JOHN. No.

MALCOLM. Look at you shaking like a shitting dog.

JOHN *pulls up his trousers*.

JOHN (*shouting*). I want to go home.

*Beat*.

Please help me.

*Beat.*

Can you help me?

*Beat.*

Somebody.

*Beat.*

MALCOLM. Go home. Please go home. Take the baby with you. There's no place like home. Is there?

*Pause.*

JOHN. No.

MALCOLM. Say it.

JOHN. There's no place like home.

MALCOLM. Louder.

JOHN. There's no place like home.

*The fluorescent light flickers and dims.*

MALCOLM. Louder.

JOHN. There's no place like home.

*Darkness.*

## Scene Three

*Two years later. Christmas. The front room of* JEAN *and* JOHN*'s house.*

*There is a white artificial Christmas tree that has seen better days.*

*It is overly decorated with an angel, mismatching tinsel, baubles and fairy lights.*

*The television is on.*

*The dark of the room is interrupted by the conflicting light from the television and the fairy lights.*

*The window is open and the fog slowly invades the front room.*

JEAN *(fifty-six) stands in the middle of the room with an apron on and some rubber washing-up gloves. She has a full milk bottle in her hand.*

JOHN *(fifty-seven) stands in the room. He is holding a suitcase.*

JEAN. A horse has just walked past our window. A horse. A big white horse. Must have got lost in the fog. You can't see a thing out there now. It came from nowhere. Just dropped out of the dark. There'll be people falling into rivers. Floating away. Singing. Old people with shopping trolleys stranded on the curbs of street corners. Pissing their pants. Kids stuck up trees. Choking on the fog.

JEAN *takes the foil top off the milk bottle and pours the milk onto the floor.*

You made me do that.

JEAN *leaves* JOHN *alone in the room.*

JEAN *comes back in with a red bucket with hot water in it.*

JEAN *takes a cloth from the bucket and wrings it out.*

*She scrubs the milk from the floor.*

I bought you a present. It's nothing much. Just something small. Just something.

JOHN *goes over to the tree and picks up the present. He shakes it.*

JOHN. What is it?

JOHN *shakes the present again. He sniffs it.*

Give me a clue.

JOHN *unwraps the present. It is a box. He lifts the lid on the box. He stares in the box.*

JEAN. I wish you hadn't opened that. You should have taken it with you. Where you are going. You should have opened it on your own.

JOHN. I didn't get you a thing.

JOHN *closes the lid of the box. He opens his suitcase on the floor and puts the box in it. He closes the case.*

You do know the window is open?

JEAN. Yes. I opened the window.

JOHN. Why did you open the window?

JEAN. Because I've not opened that window for a long time. I just wanted to see if that window still opened.

JOHN. I think I will close the window.

JOHN *goes to the window and closes it.*

*The fog continues to seep into the room, coating everything in a thin layer of mist.*

I had it all sorted out in my head. What I was going to say.

JOHN *stands in the middle of the room.*

*He does his coat up and holds the suitcase in his hand.*

*A loud thud on the window. The sound is so violent it shocks them both.*

*They both stare at each other for some time.*

JOHN *whispers.*

JEAN *doesn't.*

Did you hear that?

JEAN. Yes.

JOHN. The window?

JEAN. Yes.

JOHN. Something hit the window?

JEAN. Yes.

JOHN. Someone hit the window.

JEAN. I don't...

JOHN. Ssh.

JOHN *listens*.

I can't hear anything.

JOHN *goes to the window and looks*.

I can't see a thing.

JEAN *leaves*.

JOHN *opens the window. He steps back to safety. The fog seeps in*.

Well? Who's there? What do you want? Are you looking at me? In my own garden? Through my own window? I'm sorry if I did anything wrong. Who's there?

JOHN *stands shivering*.

JEAN *comes in carrying a dead bird*.

JEAN. It was a bird. Another one. That's three today.

JOHN. I've never thought my front-room window could be guilty of such slaughter.

JEAN. It's the fog. They don't know which way's up or down. I'll pour it down the drain.

JOHN *closes the window*.

JOHN. I'm sorry I don't love you any more, I'm sorry I won't love you again. I just don't love you. I'm just very sorry.

*Beat*.

JEAN *drops the dead bird in the bucket*.

I'm going to try and go now.

*The doorbell goes*.

*They are both still.*

We should ignore it.

*The doorbell goes again.*

They'll go away.

*The doorbell goes again but this time it is continuous.*

It's probably nothing.

JEAN *looks out of the window. Recognising who it is, she goes to the front door.*

JOHN *is left in the room alone. He straightens the angel on the Christmas tree.*

JEAN *enters followed by* NEIL *and* HELEN *(eighteen).*

NEIL *is carrying what looks like something dead in a black bin bag in his arms.*

JOHN *stares at* NEIL *and the bundle in his arms.*

NEIL *is doing his best to not cry uncontrollably. There is no hiding the raw grief he is feeling.*

HELEN *is barefoot, carrying a torch.*

NEIL. What?

JOHN *looks away.*

What you looking at?

JOHN *looks at* NEIL.

What you looking at you?

*Beat.*

My dog got run over today, John. It was a bit messy. One of its eyes was hanging out. Gunk coming out of its arse. I found Oscar and a fat little girl poking it with lolly sticks. I gave them both a crack. He was crying his eyes out. Poor fucker. I didn't want it in the first place. I knew it would end up like this. I never wanted a dog, John. But no it was always

Can we have a dog

can we have a dog

can we have a dog

can we have a dog

can we have a dog

can we have a dog

can we have a dog

Fucking stunk.

NEIL *drops the dead dog on the floor.*

Used to shit everywhere. There were always worms in it. I could have killed it myself the noise it made. I thought dogs were meant to bark. Not this fucker. It was more of a yap than a bark. I wanted to slam the car door on its head myself sometimes. I did love it though. Didn't I? Hello, John.

It's fucking shit out there. It's fucking quiet. Just the sound of hundreds of people shuffling about. Banging into phone boxes and stuff. Could we find your house? Could we fuck. Had to knock on loads of doors. No one answered except for a spastic girl eating cereal. She gave us a torch.

HELEN (*sniffing*). What's that smell?

JEAN. I can't smell anything.

HELEN (*sniffing*). Stinks.

JOHN. We had peppered mackerel for tea.

HELEN. Yes. Peppered mackerel. Stinks.

JOHN. We had it on toast. With grilled tomatoes. We always have mackerel on a Monday. You should remember that. It was your favourite.

HELEN. Yes. I do now.

NEIL. Were you going out, John?

*Beat.*

Were you going somewhere special? It's just you've got your coat on and you've got a suitcase in your hand. Where are you going on a night like this? What journey can be so important?

JOHN *puts the suitcase on the floor.*

You've had your hair done, Jean. Hasn't she, John? You have haven't you?

JEAN. I have. This morning.

NEIL. I knew it. I knew it, John. I can always tell with Jean. You look incredibly beautiful by the way.

JEAN. Thank you.

*Beat.*

We haven't seen you both for a few weeks. We've tried phoning but there was no answer. Your dad's popped round with a Christmas card but you were never in. No one.

NEIL. We've been around and about. Haven't we?

HELEN. Yes.

JOHN (*to* HELEN). You alright, love?

NEIL. What do you mean by that?

JOHN. Just asking if she's alright.

HELEN. He was just asking.

JOHN. I was just asking.

JEAN. He was just asking.

*Beat.*

JOHN. It's just you haven't got any shoes on your feet.

*Beat.*

Why haven't you got any shoes on?

HELEN. I hadn't noticed. I must have lost them. Or somebody stole them. Just disappeared in the fog. One minute they were there on my feet the next. Gone.

JOHN *picks up a pair of slippers and offers them to* HELEN.

JOHN. Here. You can have my slippers. Put them on. They
might be a bit big. But you can't walk round in this weather
with nothing on your feet. You don't know what you might
be treading on.

HELEN *puts the slippers on.*

NEIL. Right. She's good. Has her bad days, you know. Don't
you?

HELEN. Yes.

*Pause.*

NEIL (*remembering*). Fuck. A. Duck. We've left that thing in
the car. You know what I mean. That thing we got for them.
Go and get it. Go on. Tie this string round your wrist so you
can find your way back. Use the spastic's torch.

NEIL *gets a ball of string out of his pocket.*

NEIL *ties one end of the string to* HELEN*'s wrist.*

HELEN *switches on the torch and exits. The string unravels.*

NEIL, JOHN *and* JEAN *are left in the front room.*

Now you two. I want you both to close your eyes and not
open them till I tell you to. Promise me you won't peep?

JEAN *and* JOHN *both nod.*

No. No, I want you to actually promise.

JEAN *and* JOHN. Promise.

NEIL. Thank you. Go on then. Close your eyes.

JEAN *and* JOHN *close their eyes.*

No peeping, John, you little tinker. I can see you you know.

HELEN *returns with a massively oversized Christmas card
in its envelope.*

NEIL *pulls on the string, drawing her next to him.*

HELEN *remains bound at the wrist.*

You can open your eyes.

JEAN *and* JOHN *open their eyes.*

Surprise.

It's a Christmas card. We got it on the market. Are you not going to open it?

HELEN *opens the card and it begins to play a Christmas song.*

JEAN. Thank you. We'll have to find somewhere special to put it.

JEAN *takes the Christmas card and gives it to* JOHN.

NEIL. You know what I could murder now? I could murder a glass of wine. I might have a wine. Have you got any wine?

JEAN. Not open, no.

NEIL. Open us a bottle of wine, Jean. Go on. A nice bottle of Lambruscot or something. It is Christmas.

(*To* HELEN.) What do you reckon?

Helen?

HELEN. Have what you want don't you. At Christmas.

NEIL *gets lost in his own head for a few seconds.*

*It's as though his brain has been switched off and back on again.*

*It's like a computer rebooting after a fault.*

JOHN, JEAN *and* HELEN *stand silently.*

NEIL *is like a bomb waiting to explode.*

NEIL. Wine? What on its own?

HELEN. Yeah, I think so.

NEIL. Right. Can I have a glass of wine? Please. Jean.

JEAN *looks at* JOHN.

JOHN *nods.*

JEAN *goes to get the wine leaving* JOHN, HELEN *and* NEIL *in the front room.*

*Silence.*

NEIL *looks at the TV.*

*He smiles.*

'*Cold Outside*' *is being performed by Dean Martin. A Christmas special or something.*

I love this song. Turn it up.

JOHN *turns the volume up on the TV.*

NEIL *grabs hold of* HELEN.

*He begins to dance.*

*He sings.*

JOHN *watches awkwardly.*

JEAN *returns with a glass of wine.*

*She stands in the doorway watching* NEIL *and* HELEN *dance.*

*When* NEIL *notices* JEAN *and the glass of wine he dances* HELEN *over to* JOHN.

*He gives his daughter to him.*

*He makes them dance.*

NEIL *goes to* JEAN *and takes the glass of wine and downs it. He takes hold of* JEAN *and the two begin to dance.*

*The four of them dance around the dead dog on the floor.*

*The string on* HELEN's *wrist creates a web that surrounds them as they dance.*

*The song ends.*

HELEN *kicks the bin bag*.

Nothing lasts for ever. I told Oscar you would help him bury it
in the back garden under the tree. Make a cross out of scraps
of wood. You've got a smart garden. Vegetable patch. Flowers.
Roses. Better than ours. Our dead garden. You should make a
swing for him. He'd like that. Make him a sandpit. Fill it with
soil. He'd like that. Will you bury him, Dad?

JOHN. Yes.

HELEN. Promise.

JOHN. I promise.

HELEN. We could get him a bucket and spade. Pretend he's on
holiday.

NEIL. He'll pretend to be a builder, making houses out of mud.
He likes playing doesn't he?

HELEN. Yes.

NEIL. He's like a little creature when he's playing.

HELEN. Like a little worm-boy always digging. Dirty little
fingernails.

NEIL. We need you to look after Oscar for a while. Let him live
here for a bit.

JOHN. It's not a good time at the moment. It really isn't. Is it?

JEAN *looks down*.

NEIL. It was her idea. Isn't that right?

HELEN *looks down*.

Isn't it?

HELEN. Yes.

JEAN. I'll just go and say hello to him.

NEIL. It's cold out there. Don't want to be poorly for Christmas
do you, Jean? Who'd cook John's turkey? Eh? Gobble
gobble gobble.

JEAN. I'll put my coat on.

HELEN. He's asleep.

JEAN. I'll go and have a look. Just in case.

NEIL. You can't see a thing out there now.

JEAN. I'll use your torch.

NEIL *stamps on the torch until it breaks*.

HELEN. It's broken.

*Pause*.

JOHN. I think it's getting out of hand all of this. It is. I think...

NEIL. I'd rather shit in my hands and clap than listen to what you think.

JOHN. You don't intimidate me. You don't scare me. This is my house. I've lived here for a very long time. And I won't have your type trying to do what you're trying to do. I'm no walkover. You need to know that.

NEIL. You should sit down. You're getting overexcited.

JOHN. I'm quite happy where I am thank you.

NEIL. Sit down.

JOHN. No. I think I want to stand.

NEIL. I think you should sit down.

JOHN. I don't care what you think. I'm standing. I'm making a stand.

NEIL. You should tell him.

HELEN. Please sit down, Dad.

JOHN. I have no intention of sitting down. I might even stand for ever.

NEIL. I swear to fucking Jesus Christ if you don't sit down right now I'm going to stick my cock right up your little girl's fanny right here in this front room in front of her mummy and daddy. Sit down.

*Beat.*

JOHN. You're calling my bluff.

NEIL. Take your knickers off and give them to Mummy to hold.

HELEN *takes her knickers off and gives them to* JEAN.

JEAN. I think it would be best if you just sat down now.

JOHN *defiantly stands*.

NEIL. I fuck your little girl until she screams and begs me to stop.

*Beat.*

Do you understand?

*Beat.*

Do you get me?

JEAN. –

NEIL. Don't interrupt, Jean. It will only drag this out. I do things to your daughter, John, that you could only wank about –

JEAN (*whispering*). Get out –

NEIL. Sometimes I let my mates do your daughter one after the other –

JEAN (*quietly*). Get out –

NEIL. She can't open her legs fast enough –

JOHN. Shut your mouth –

NEIL. She'd shag you if I told her to –

JOHN *slowly sits*.

Now stay sat down, John. Don't even think about getting up. I want you to sit in that chair and think about what you just did and when you think you can be a good little boy you can join in the adult conversation with me and Jean.

JEAN. I've got money upstairs.

NEIL. I don't want money.

JEAN. I can get more.

NEIL. How much? What she worth?

JEAN *gets an envelope from her handbag.*

JEAN. There's thirty-five pounds and some coins in there. I want you to take it.

JEAN *passes the envelope to* NEIL.

NEIL *opens the envelope and takes the money out of it.*

NEIL. Right.

NEIL *rips the money in half and throws it in* JEAN*'s face.*

I don't want your money, Jean. Did you not listen to what I said? I will say it very, very slowly.

*Beat.*

We want. Oscar. Your grandson. To come here. To this house. And live. With you. Two. Happily. Ever. After. We don't want him. (*To* HELEN.) Do we? You don't want him. Do you? Tell them.

(*Murderously.*) Please tell them.

HELEN. I wish he was dead. Why didn't I let him die when he was born? Put him out of all this misery. I should've drowned him in that canal. Cut him up to bits with a knife and fork. Fed him to stray dogs. I should've stabbed him through the head with thin knitting needles. Pierced his brain. Popped his head with bricks. Poured concrete in his nose and mouth. Painted him black and sank him in mud. He makes me feel dirty that he came from me. That he grew inside me. Feeding off me. Chewing on my insides. Taking me over. Stripping the layers off me from the inside out. Poisoning me. Killing me. Turning me into a ruin. A woman who doesn't know how to love. I remember nothing. Why can't he be dead?

NEIL. The worse it is the more you've got to laugh. Now are we all ready to compromise for a bit of freedom, because I don't want this chaos any more?

*Beat.*

That's a really nice tree.

HELEN. Go and get Oscar from the car, Dad.

JOHN *gets up, leaves the room.*

JEAN *drops the knickers on the floor.*

JEAN *picks up the suitcase and leaves the room.*

HELEN *picks the knickers and puts them on.*

HELEN *straightens the angel on top of the Christmas tree.*

I love you.

**Scene Four**

*Two years later. The end of August. The sand dunes at Blackpool.*

*It is late afternoon on a quiet and secluded part of the seafront.*

*It is muggy and the sun keeps disappearing behind the clouds. There will be a storm later. The faint sound of the amusement arcades and the Pleasure Beach can be heard in the distance.*

JEAN (*fifty-eight*) *is sat on a deckchair.*

*She looks through a telescope.*

JOHN (*fifty-nine*) *is a few feet away from her. All we can see is his head poking out of the sand. He has been buried up to his neck.*

*A bucket and spade are discarded at his feet and two glittery windmills on sticks are stuck in the sand. They are slightly turning in the breeze.*

*A pair of children's socks and shoes are placed neatly by the bucket.*

OSCAR (*six*) *is playing on a part of the beach some way away. We can't see him.*

JEAN. He's kissing that young girl.

JOHN. Who is?

JEAN. That man from the chip shop. The one who shared our table.

JOHN. The one who ate all our bread and butter?

JEAN. Yes. Him. He's got his hands all over that young girl who gives the change out at the amusement arcade. The one with the boy's haircut and the gammy hand.

JOHN. Smarmy bugger. I knew there was something about him. You can always tell a lot about a man from how much salt and vinegar he puts on his chips. Flamboyance with condiments smacks of depravity. That's what my dad used to say.

*Pause.*

What they doing now?

JEAN. They keep looking round to see if anyone can see them. I don't think she wants to be seen.

JOHN. I don't bloody blame the poor cow. I bet he's diseased with God knows what. Riddled. Did you see the way he was eating. Got more on his face than in his mouth. Bits of batter in his sideburns.

JEAN. They're lying down on the sand. He's using her overall as a pillow.

JOHN. He's a parasite.

JEAN. She's stroking his face.

JOHN. I hope she washes her hands.

JEAN. She's resting her chin on his beer belly.

JOHN. Is she looking him in the eye?

JEAN. She's very beautiful.

JOHN. Is she looking at him in the eye?

JEAN. He's closed his eyes.

JOHN. Scum.

*Pause.*

What they doing now?

JEAN. Holding.

JOHN. She's teasing him. That's what it will be. She'll have made a bet with the girls she works with in the arcade.

JEAN. She's very attentive. She looks very experienced for such a young girl.

JOHN. What's she doing to him?

*Pause.*

What's she done?

JEAN. She's watching him sleep.

JOHN. Sleep? Not very likely. He's probably died. That's what it is. That's what it will be. A mortality on the beach. How very embarrassing. They'll have to drag his fat pustulated carcass off the sand. With ropes and a tractor. Like a dead sea creature covered in sewage and seaweed. String him up on the promenade. Cut him open. Like a prized shark. Let all his secrets splatter on the ground. I'll take my bread and butter back thank you very much.

JEAN. He's snoozing. He's not dead. He's just snoozing. I can see him breathing. He's dreaming.

JOHN. Well… we'll see.

Where's Oscar? He's not near them is he?

JEAN. No. He's over there. Stroking donkeys.

JOHN. Good. Out of my sight. He played up like a right bloody
lunatic in that toy shop. Out of control he was.
Embarrassing. Going mad because I wouldn't buy him a
cowboy costume. I wouldn't mind but I'd already bought
him a plastic sword. And a gun. Bloody shouting. Swearing.
Hitting me with that sword right across my face. Nearly had
my sodding eye out. Nearly bloody blinded me. I grabbed
hold of his arm. I pulled his pants right down to his ankles
and I belted him as hard as I could on his arse. If I say he
can't have something he can't have it.

*A bird shits on* JOHN*'s head.*

A bird has just shit on me.

*Beat.*

A bird has just shit on my head.

JEAN. Good for you.

JOHN. What?

JEAN. I said it's good for you. It's good luck. That's what
they've always said. If a bird… poos on you it's good luck.

JOHN *looks at* JEAN.

JEAN *looks at* JOHN.

It's always been like that. For ever.

JOHN (*incredulous*). What? I don't care if it's good luck or not.
I've got birdshit on my head and I want you to wipe it off,
Jean. That's if you don't think it's too much trouble.

JEAN. I don't know if I can do that. It might cancel out the luck.

JOHN. What?

JEAN. We could do with some good luck.

JOHN. Just wipe it off my head. Jean. Please.

*JEAN gets up.*

*JEAN switches off her fan and puts it down.*

*JEAN gets a tissue out of her pocket and goes over to JOHN.*

JEAN. It's only a little bit. Must have been a small bird. A baby or something.

*JEAN wraps up the tissue and puts it in the bucket.*

*JEAN goes back to her chair, picks up the fan, switches it on and sits down.*

JOHN. Thank you.

*A distant rumble of thunder is heard in the distance. A dog barks.*

JEAN. I love it here. I love the beach. I love the sand between my toes. If I close my eyes I'm a little girl again. I can almost feel my mother next to me. I can hear my dad breathing. I can smell them. I can hear my mum laughing. I really can. I think this is the happiest place in the world. If I close my eyes life doesn't exist any more.

JOHN. We'll have to go soon. It's going to rain. I can smell it.

JEAN. You're always saying it's going to rain. It never does. You're not very good with the weather.

*Beat.*

JOHN. It's cold.

JEAN. It's not. It's warm. I dripped ice cream onto my dress. It must be hot. I hope the raspberry sauce doesn't stain. I can always try and take it back. I've kept the bag and the receipt.

*The windmills stuck in the sand begin to spin faster.*

*It thunders again.*

JOHN. What time is it?

JEAN *ignores* JOHN.

Look at the state of that sky. It's gone black.

*Beat.*

It feels like we've been here for hours. How long's it been? It must be at least an hour.

JEAN. It isn't.

JOHN. We must have been. My arse has gone numb. And my legs. I can't feel a thing. Nothing. Anything could be going on down there. I haven't got a bloody clue. I feel like one of them paraplegics.

JEAN. We've only been in here for twenty minutes. (*Looking at her watch.*) Thirty-five minutes.

*Beat.*

Always exaggerating.

JEAN *gets up.*

JEAN *stretches.*

OSCAR *shouts from a different part of the beach.*

OSCAR (*offstage*). Nana. Nana.

JEAN *looks through the telescope.*

Look. I found it.

JEAN. Oscar's found a kite.

JOHN. What colour?

JEAN. Red.

OSCAR (*offstage*). Can I keep it?

JEAN. Be careful.

JEAN *goes back to the deckchair and sits down.*

*A rumble of thunder is heard. This time it is closer.*

JOHN. Was that thunder?

*Beat.*

Was that thunder, Jean?

*Beat.*

JEAN (*not listening to what he said*). What's the matter with you?

JOHN. I didn't want to come to Blackpool in the first place. It's horrible. Grotty. Stinks of egg. Everywhere stinks of egg. The sea doesn't even like coming here.

*Beat.*

And a bird has shit on my head.

JEAN. You're a right miserable sod.

JOHN. I'm not.

JEAN. You are, John. The only chance we get to get away for a few days and all you do is moan.

JOHN. I don't.

JEAN. You do.

*Beat.*

A bit of poo never hurt anyone.

*Pause.*

JOHN. How long do I have to stay like this for? I can't feel my toes any more.

*A rumble of thunder is heard. The storm is getting closer.*

You should keep an eye on Oscar. He can disappear just like that.

*JEAN looks through the telescope.*

JEAN. I can only just see him. I think that kite's too big for him. It's lifting him off the ground.

*JEAN shouts to OSCAR who is now quite far away.*

Oscar.

*Beat.*

Oscar.

*Beat.*

Let go of it. You'll get blown away if you're not careful.

*Pause.*

Can you remember when we brought his mum here when she was little? That red-hot summer. You got sunburnt that bad you had to sleep in a bath full of cold water. Nearly bloody killed yourself, daft sod. You lost her in the arcades.

JOHN. I didn't.

JEAN. You bloody did. I was playing bingo and you said you would take her to play on the two-pence machines that she liked.

JOHN. I can't remember that.

JEAN. You did, John. You lost her.

*Beat.*

She was gone for a few hours. You must remember.

*Beat.*

JOHN. She always had a good sense of direction.

JEAN. You wanted to tell the police then we found her in Woolworths. She'd walked up to the manager's office and told him she was lost.

*Beat.*

I can't believe you don't remember. He'd given her a packet of Rolos to stop her crying. She'd lost her shoes. She wouldn't talk to you for days.

JOHN. That blue pair with dogs on?

JEAN. No, not the ones with the dogs on. The red ones. The red ones with the gold writing on the bottom. You spent a whole day going all over trying to find a pair. She never forgot that.

JOHN. Didn't she?

*Beat.*

JEAN. No. She never forgot that.

*It starts to spit with rain.*

*The storm is on top of them now.*

*It's incredibly still.*

*It is black.*

It's spitting.

*Pause.*

JOHN. How do you lose your shoes? I don't understand. A shoe in the road. On a wall. Floating in the canal. Where do they all come from? I don't understand it. Do you?

*Beat.*

That dead girl I found. She had no shoes on. Funny what you forget. How you remember.

JEAN *gets a small hand-held umbrella out and raises it.*

JEAN *looks for* OSCAR.

JEAN. I can hardly see him. He's just a dot on the horizon.

JOHN. She had no arms. I thought it was her. I was convinced it was our Helen. On a dirty mattress with ants everywhere.

JEAN (*shouting*). Oscar, come on now it's starting to rain.

JOHN. I wanted to touch her.

JEAN (*picking up his shoes and socks*). Your socks will get all wet.

JOHN. I wanted to protect her. I wanted to wrap her up in a blanket and tell her she was alright, that everything would be okay. I wanted to stroke her hair and sing her to sleep. What she must have gone through.

JEAN. Come on, Oscar, I'm not messing now. Your shoes are getting wet.

JOHN. I just stood there being sick through my hands at a dead girl with hair but no face.

*It flashes with lightning and a loud rumble of thunder briefly follows.*

JEAN. Oscar. Hurry up.

JEAN *takes off her sunhat and sunglasses and puts them in her bag.*

JOHN. She'd started to rot.

JEAN. You'll get struck by lightning, Oscar, and that will really hurt.

JOHN. She'd started to melt. She was disappearing into death. It became her. Life was giving her back. She was more than the thing she was.

JEAN. I'm going to leave your bucket and spade here.

JOHN. And in that moment I spent with the dead girl I felt a closeness and love that I've never had with my own daughter.

JEAN. Come on, Oscar, don't ruin a good day.

JOHN. I will always remember everything about that girl in death. Why can't I remember my own daughter in life?

JEAN. I'm not joking, Oscar, you'll catch your death.

JEAN *goes off to get* OSCAR.

JOHN *is left alone.*

*It thunders really loud.*

JOHN. A father should remember he lost his little girl. He should remember what colour her shoes were.

*The sky darkens.*

## Scene Five

*Two years later. The final day of autumn. A wood on the edge of a graveyard.*

*Late afternoon. Dusk approaches.*

*Mottled sunshine dances through the treetops casting rippling puddles of light on the ground.*

*The chatter of leaves and shy birdsong fills the clearing.*

OSCAR (*eight*) *is looking at the tops of the trees through a small telescope.*

*He is wearing a pair of red wellington boots.*

*His bike leans against an old forgotten bench.*

PHILIP *is sat on the bench.*

*He watches* OSCAR *silently.*

*After some time.*

PHILIP. I don't know much about birds.

   OSCAR *is still.*

   Is that terrible?

   OSCAR *is still.*

   I wish I did.

   OSCAR *is still.*

   I wish I'd paid them more attention.

   OSCAR *is still.*

   Do you mind me sitting here?

   OSCAR *is still.*

I've never had a telescope. I always wanted one. When I was a boy I really wanted a telescope. My insides used to ache I wanted one so much. I remember that feeling. Its taste in my mouth. The things I imagined I could've seen if only I'd had a telescope. The faces I might have captured. Eyes glistening. Upturned smiles. Arms outstretched and wanting. Touching me from a distance I couldn't quite reach. I never had a telescope. Hello. Can you hear me? I'm sorry.

OSCAR *is still.*

PHILIP *takes a small bird whistle from his bag.*

*He plays it quietly.*

OSCAR *watches* PHILIP.

PHILIP *is embarrassed.*

*He stops playing the whistle.*

*He wipes the corners of his mouth.*

*He smiles.*

*He offers the whistle to* OSCAR.

OSCAR *hesitates.*

*He looks back to the tops of the trees through his telescope.*

PHILIP *places the whistle on the bench next to him.*

*He looks up into the trees.*

*He shields his eyes from the sun.*

OSCAR. That's a chiffchaff.

*Beat.*

Where you're looking. It's a chiffchaff. It lives in that tree.

*Beat.*

It looks like a willow warbler but not as yellow.

PHILIP. They all look the same to me.

PHILIP *opens his bag and takes out a plastic sandwich box.*

*He opens it and takes out a sandwich.*

*He offers the sandwich to* OSCAR.

Would you like a cheese sandwich?

*Beat.*

OSCAR. I don't like cheese.

PHILIP. Everyone likes cheese.

OSCAR *looks at* PHILIP.

OSCAR. I don't. It's yellow. Stinks of cow tits.

OSCAR *turns away and looks back up into the trees.*

PHILIP. Do you mind if I have one?

OSCAR *shakes his head.*

PHILIP *eats the sandwich.*

*He brushes the crumbs from his clothes.*

OSCAR. Would you like to look through my telescope?

OSCAR *offers the telescope to* PHILIP.

There aren't many birds here today. The rooks have scared most of them away. I hate rooks.

*Beat.*

PHILIP. Thank you.

PHILIP *takes the telescope and looks into the trees.*

OSCAR *takes a small book from one of his wellington boots.*

OSCAR. My nana bought me this book at a jumble sale. It was only five pence. When I see a bird I tick it off. There were already a lot of ticks in it when I got it but I just rubbed them out. Started again. Bargain.

*Beat.*

PHILIP. Do you spend a lot of time here?

OSCAR. Sometimes.

PHILIP. Me too.

PHILIP *lowers the telescope and offers it back to* OSCAR.

I think I've seen you here before. You haven't seen me but I think I've seen you.

*Beat.*

You're always alone.

*Beat.*

Do your friends not like looking at birds?

OSCAR. I have got friends. Loads of friends.

PHILIP. I'm sure you have.

OSCAR. About one hundred.

PHILIP. Good.

*Pause.*

Can I see your book?

OSCAR. Do you like birds?

PHILIP. I think so yes.

OSCAR *isn't sure if he should let* PHILIP *see the book.*

I do. I don't know much about them but I do like them.

OSCAR. Spell albatross.

PHILIP (*struggling*). A.L.B.A.T.R.O.S.S.

OSCAR *passes the book to the man.*

(*Reading the title.*) '*A Pocket Guide to Birds.*'

PHILIP *flicks through the book.*

You've seen a lot of birds. There are a lot of ticks.

OSCAR. My granddad has seen most of them. He's ticked off
most of them. I've ticked off quite a few though.

PHILIP. Your granddad comes birdwatching with you?

OSCAR. Sometimes.

PHILIP. Does he?

*Beat.*

Is he here today?

OSCAR. No, he's at home.

PHILIP *sits on the bench.*

*He plays the bird whistle quietly.*

OSCAR *watches him.*

*He looks back to the tops of the trees through his telescope.*

Do you know what my name is?

PHILIP *stops playing the whistle.*

PHILIP. No. I don't. Would you like me to know your name?

*Beat.*

I think I'd like to know your name.

*Beat.*

What's your name?

OSCAR *looks at* PHILIP.

OSCAR. You'll never guess.

PHILIP. I might.

OSCAR. You won't. It's too hard.

*Beat.*

PHILIP. I bet you a go of my bird whistle I do.

PHILIP *stands.*

OSCAR *hesitates.*

*OSCAR looks at his bike.*

OSCAR. I bet you a go of my bike you don't.

*They stand opposite each other.*

Three guesses. That's the rule. Agreed?

PHILIP. Agreed.

*OSCAR holds out three fingers as markers.*

OSCAR. Go on then.

*Pause.*

PHILIP. Robert.

OSCAR. No.

*OSCAR lowers one of his fingers.*

Two chances left.

PHILIP *inhales a large breath.*

PHILIP. Ian?

OSCAR. Wrong.

*OSCAR lowers another finger leaving one remaining.*

Last guess.

PHILIP. Simon.

*OSCAR lowers his final finger.*

OSCAR. No. You lose.

PHILIP *smiles.*

PHILIP *holds out the bird whistle.*

My name is Oscar.

*OSCAR slowly walks over to PHILP.*

*They both hold the bird whistle.*

*They hold each other's stare.*

My nana says it's very distinguished.

PHILIP. It is.

*PHILIP lets go of the bird whistle.*

*OSCAR retreats.*

You win, Oscar.

*OSCAR quietly plays the bird whistle.*

*He stops.*

*OSCAR returns the bird whistle to the bench.*

OSCAR. I don't have one hundred friends. I lied. I don't have any friends.

*Beat.*

I'm too selfish.

*Beat.*

That's what my granddad says.

*Beat.*

PHILIP. I don't think you're selfish.

*PHILIP sits on the bench.*

*He takes a bottle of suncream from his bag and begins to apply it to his arms.*

You let me look through your telescope. I don't think a selfish person would do that. I think that's kind. That is kindness, Oscar. I appreciate it. Thank you.

*Beat.*

I come here just to look at the trees like you just come to look at the birds. I'm never disappointed because they are always here. They never go away. They change and grow but they're always here. Constant. I appreciate that.

I sometimes imagine that these are the only trees left in the world and that every single bird has to come here to make its nest. Silly isn't it. But if you think like that then you start to see them differently. It makes you really appreciate them the way I do you and the way your granddad should too.

*Beat.*

I think your granddad is wrong.

*The sun goes behind a cloud.*

*The sun has gone in.*

*Everything is grey.*

*The world has stopped.*

*They both look up at the sky.*

OSCAR. It's like looking at another galaxy. I think it looks beautiful. My granddad says grey clouds are bad.

PHILIP. Does he?

OSCAR. I don't. I think if you really look at them they're never really just grey. The sky seems more important when the sun goes behind a cloud. I don't know why. It's more hopeful.

  OSCAR *looks at* PHILIP *who continues looking at the sky.*

We could be friends.

PHILIP. I'm not sure. I don't really know you.

OSCAR. You know my name.

  PHILIP *looks at* OSCAR.

PHILIP. What do you think my name is?

OSCAR. I don't know.

  PHILIP *laughs quietly.*

PHILIP. If you can guess my name you can keep my bird whistle. But if you don't you've got to give me something in return.

OSCAR. Like what?

  PHILIP *shrugs his shoulders.*

You can't have my telescope. It's priceless.

*Beat.*

PHILIP. I don't want your telescope.

OSCAR. You can't have my bike either.

PHILIP. I don't want your bike.

OSCAR. I haven't got anything else.

*Pause.*

PHILIP. I know.

OSCAR. What?

PHILIP. No...

OSCAR. What?

PHILIP. It's silly.

OSCAR. What?

*Beat.*

PHILIP. Promise you won't laugh?

OSCAR. I promise.

PHILIP. If you don't guess my name... If you don't guess my name... you've got to...

*Beat.*

You've got to take your shorts off and you've got to sit on my knee.

*Beat.*

OSCAR. I don't think I want to take my shorts off. I don't think I want to sit on your knee.

PHILIP. I don't want you to sit on my knee either. I don't even know you, Oscar. It's just a bet. It's a game. It's what friends do.

If you don't want to win the bird whistle then...

PHILIP *picks up the bird whistle.*

If you don't want to be friends...

PHILIP *picks up his bag.*

If you don't think you can guess…

PHILIP *stands and goes to leave.*

Goodbye, Oscar.

OSCAR. Okay.

PHILIP. Good boy.

PHILIP *returns to the bench and sits down.*

*He puts the bird whistle on the bench.*

You've got three guesses.

PHILIP *holds out three fingers as markers.*

OSCAR *concentrates.*

OSCAR. Tom.

PHILIP. Wrong. Two more guesses.

PHILIP *lowers one of his fingers.*

OSCAR. Neil?

PHILIP. Wrong. Last guess.

PHILIP *lowers another finger, leaving one remaining.*

OSCAR *closes his eyes.*

*The sun comes out.*

OSCAR. Philip.

OSCAR *opens his eyes.*

Your name is Philip.

*Pause.*

PHILIP. Yes.

I am called Philip.

PHILIP *holds the bird whistle out to* OSCAR.

Good guess.

OSCAR. I'm good at guessing things.

PHILIP. You are aren't you?

OSCAR. I always have been.

OSCAR *takes the bird whistle*.

PHILIP. I didn't know I was playing with an expert.

OSCAR. I know your wife's name as well.

PHILIP. What?

OSCAR. I know what your wife's called.

PHILIP. I'm not married.

OSCAR. Yes you are.

PHILIP. No. I'm not.

OSCAR. Your wife is called Carol.

OSCAR *has correctly named* PHILIP*'s wife*.

PHILIP. No... Oscar... wrong... You're wrong this time...
wrong I'm not married.

OSCAR. And you have a daughter. Called Karen.

*Beat*.

PHILIP. What?

OSCAR. She's very poorly. She cries a lot. She's dying.

PHILIP (*lying and confused by* OSCAR*'s clairvoyance*). No...
No... Not right... No no no, that's wrong no, wrong. Do you
know me... Oscar?

OSCAR. No.

PHILIP. Did you guess we'd be friends?

OSCAR *looks at* PHILIP *and smiles*.

OSCAR. Yes.

PHILIP. Good.

PHILIP *offers* OSCAR *his hand*.

OSCAR *doesn't offer his.*

Pleased to meet you, Oscar.

PHILIP *offers his hand for an uncomfortable amount of time.*

OSCAR *looks at the offered hand.*

OSCAR *looks through his telescope into the trees.*

PHILIP *sits on the bench.*

*He looks at* OSCAR.

PHILIP *takes the bottle of suncream out of his bag.*

*He places it on the bench next to him.*

*He looks up at the sky, shielding his eyes from the sun.*

*He looks at* OSCAR.

*He picks up the suncream and squeezes a small amount into his hand.*

*He rubs the suncream into his legs.*

I think I've burnt my neck.

*Beat.*

Oscar.

OSCAR. Yes.

PHILIP. I think I've burnt my neck.

*Beat.*

I hope you've got some suntan cream on.

OSCAR. What?

PHILIP. The sun is really strong when it gets through the trees.
You don't want to burn.

OSCAR. I won't.

PHILIP. You don't want to die of cancer. Shall I rub some
cream in for you?

OSCAR. No thank you.

*Pause.*

PHILIP. I think my neck is burning.

*Beat.*

Is it red?

OSCAR *looks at* PHILIP'*s neck.*

OSCAR. No. It's alright.

PHILIP. It feels very burnt.

OSCAR. It's not.

*Pause.*

PHILIP. Will you rub some cream into my neck?

OSCAR *looks at* PHILIP.

*They hold each other's stare.*

OSCAR. Would you like me to?

PHILIP. Yes. I think I would like that. It's probably for the best.

OSCAR *goes to* PHILIP.

OSCAR *picks up the bottle of suncream.*

OSCAR *shakes the bottle.*

OSCAR *squeezes some of the cream into his hand.*

OSCAR *puts the bottle on the bench.*

OSCAR *rubs his hands together.*

PHILIP *lowers his head exposing his neck.*

OSCAR *rubs the cream into* PHILIP'*s neck.*

OSCAR *sits on his bike.*

OSCAR *starts to leave.*

OSCAR *stops.*

*OSCAR gets off his bike and puts the bird whistle back on the bench.*

*OSCAR gets back on his bike.*

OSCAR. I'm sorry.

PHILIP. I know.

*OSCAR leaves on his bike.*

*PHILIP is left alone.*

*After a very brief time, OSCAR returns on his bike.*

*In his hand is a doll. It has fallen out of a child's pushchair.*

*OSCAR offers PHILIP the doll.*

OSCAR. Do you want this?

*Beat.*

I found it in the leaves.

*Beat.*

It's not dirty. Someone must have just lost it.

*Beat.*

I thought you could give it to your little girl.

*Beat.*

I think she would like it.

*Beat.*

I think she would appreciate it.

*OSCAR goes to PHILIP.*

*OSCAR offers PHILIP the doll.*

*PHILIP looks at OSCAR.*

*PHILIP looks at the doll.*

*PHILIP takes the doll.*

I know you're not a bad person. You're not.

*Beat.*

Philip?

PHILIP. Yes.

OSCAR. I hope your little girl gets better. I really do. I hope she stops crying soon.

PHILIP. Thank you, Oscar. Goodbye.

OSCAR. Goodbye, Philip.

PHILIP *stands.*

PHILIP *wipes his eyes.*

PHILIP *puts the suncream into his bag.*

PHILIP *picks up the bird whistle.*

PHILIP *leaves.*

OSCAR *circles the clearing on his bike.*

*The birdsong gets louder and all the leaves fall from the trees.*

OSCAR *leaves the clearing.*


## Scene Six

*Two years later. The first day of spring. JEAN and JOHN's back garden.*

*The sounds of the first grass-cut of the year.*

*Lawnmowers and dogs. A semi-distant crying baby.*

*JOHN (sixty-three) is in the middle of the garden.*

*He is in the process of building something that resembles a bird stand.*

OSCAR *(ten) is helping construct the bird stand.*

OSCAR *is wearing a World War II tin helmet and carrying a hammer.*

*A radio is playing in the background.*

OSCAR *listens to the music.*

OSCAR *begins to dance.*

JOHN *tries not to watch.*

OSCAR. I can't believe we had a bloody earthquake, Granddad.

JOHN. What've I told you about swearing?

OSCAR. Bloody isn't a swear word, Granddad.

JOHN. It is.

*Beat.*

It wasn't an earthquake anyway. Just a bloody big tremor.

OSCAR. Everything in my classroom started to shake. Even my fat teacher. You could see her big fat face wobbling. I thought the roof was going to fall on my head and smash my brains in. All the windows explode in people's faces. People fall down holes of fire in the floor. Legs squashed flat like toilet paper. The ground might just swallow us all up. I hope it does. I can't decide now whether the world is going to end with a massive earthquake or a big nuclear war. I don't know which one's best.

*Beat.*

I'm going to wear this hat now forever just in case.

OSCAR *hits himself on the head repeatedly with the hammer.*

*It makes a tune and he dances.*

You know the first thing that happens when a nuclear bomb explodes. There's a massive flash and it can melt your eyes if you look at it. Your skin can set on fire and start to bubble up. Most people are dead straight away. But some people are left without anyone to look after them because everyone they know is dead and they start being sick and bits of their stomach start coming out of their mouths. Your head starts to die and all your hair falls out and you go bald like a granddad. You can't eat anything because it's all poisoned so you start to turn into a skeleton and your gums and your mouth and throat start to bleed. Then you get the runs all the time and you can't stop pooing your pants and when you've run out of poo your insides start to fall out of your bum. Then you die.

JOHN (*concentrating on the bird stand*). Who told you that?

OSCAR. My dad. He said it's going to happen soon.

JOHN (*ignoring* OSCAR). Did he?

OSCAR. He said that I would be at school and the air-raid siren would go off and I would only have three minutes left to live.

JOHN (*ignoring* OSCAR). Did he?

OSCAR. If it happened on a Thursday Nana would be shopping in the Co-op so I bet she would die. You'd be alright cos you could just hide in next door's old air-raid shelter.

JOHN. Oscar.

OSCAR. You'd have to stay in there for ages. I think you will still die though.

JOHN. Oscar, will you shut your face for a bit. You don't know what you're talking about. We need to finish your bird stand.

OSCAR *goes to his bird stand and starts to work on it.*

OSCAR. I do know what I'm talking about you know. My dad tells me all about it when I go to see him.

JOHN. Give me that hammer.

OSCAR. Granddad, do you think about the day you will die?

JOHN. Only when I spend a lot of time with you.

OSCAR *opens the tin of paint. He dips his brush in and starts to paint the bird stand.*

OSCAR. I think about the day I'm going to die and I think about that day all the time. You're an old man which means you must think about the day you're going to die a lot more than I do.

JOHN. You don't know the day you're going to die, Oscar, nobody does, not even your nana and she knows everything. If we all knew the day we were going to die then the world would stop. Nobody would do anything.

*Pause.*

Did you get the bus to see Dad?

OSCAR. Yeah.

JOHN. Did you have to wait again to see him?

OSCAR. We always do but the man Nana talks to gets me a hot chocolate from the machine in the waiting room.

JOHN. Does he?

OSCAR. He's always there when we're there. We always see the same people in that room.

JOHN. Do you?

OSCAR. The man sits next to me. He talks to Nana but he sits next to me.

JOHN. Your nana speaks to all the strange people. It's the same when we go to the dentist. She attracts them. She's like a magnet for weirdos.

OSCAR. I don't think he's weird I just think he's lonely.

*Pause.*

JOHN. So what do they talk about your nana and this man?

OSCAR. I don't think I'm meant to listen.

JOHN. I bet you do.

*Beat.*

It's human nature to do things we're not meant to do.

*Beat.*

Like picking your nose.

OSCAR. I pick my nose all the time, Granddad. Does that mean that I'm allowed to do anything I want even though it might be wrong?

JOHN. No, Oscar, I'm just saying that sometimes we have to choose. You're not meant to pick your nose because other people don't like seeing you pick your nose. But if you pick your nose when no one is looking it doesn't really matter.

OSCAR. I think I understand, Granddad.

JOHN. So what do they talk about?

OSCAR. They talk quite quietly. He cries sometimes.

JOHN. Your nana never mentioned she spoke to a man at the hospital. Not a man that cried anyway.

OSCAR. They all do in that room. One starts and then they all start.

JOHN. There's a lot of brokenness in the world, Oscar. A lot of people find themselves drawn together without knowing it and end up sharing things they wouldn't normally dream of doing. That room is like a Hoover sucking them all together.

OSCAR. All you can hear is the whispers. I think it's a bit rude. I get told off by my big fat teacher for whispering. You don't get children whispering like that, Granddad.

JOHN. If I was you, Oscar, next time I was there I would turn round to this man and say – 'Excuse me, my teacher said it is rude to whisper.'

OSCAR. I don't think Nana would be very happy if I said that to her friend. It might make him cry and then Nana would have to hold his hand again.

*Beat.*

Nana never holds my hand. When I cry Nana never holds my hand.

*Beat.*

Does Nana ever hold your hand, Granddad? When you cry does she hold your hand?

JOHN. No she never holds my hand.

OSCAR. Why does she hold hands with a man she doesn't know?

*Beat.*

Why can't she hold hands with me or you?

*Beat.*

She knows me and you better than that crying man in the hospital waiting room.

JOHN. I think your nana would love to hold your hand.

OSCAR. I don't think she does.

JOHN. I think that is what she most wants in the whole world.

OSCAR. I think you know that isn't true, Granddad.

JOHN. Sometimes we can't touch the people we care and love the most because we just don't know how to do it. It just feels wrong.

OSCAR. I'm ten. I think I know how to hold hands.

JOHN. You're lucky. It's been taken from us. We've lost it.

*Pause.*

So how is your dad?

OSCAR. I was enjoying talking to you about life, Granddad.

JOHN. He's a very sick man your dad, Oscar.

*Beat.*

Does he still stink of shit?

*Beat.*

Does he still try and touch himself when you talk to him?

*Beat.*

Does he still not know who you are?

Have you ever wondered why he doesn't recognise you, Oscar? Why he never remembers your name?

OSCAR. He had an accident when I was small.

JOHN. He didn't have an accident, Oscar.

OSCAR. He fell off a crane.

JOHN. He didn't fall off a crane, Oscar.

OSCAR. He did. He worked on the world's biggest crane. That's how he damaged his brain.

JOHN. He never worked on a crane. He never worked. It was a story we made up to stop you asking stupid questions.

OSCAR. Stop it, Granddad.

JOHN. He jumped off a bridge in front of a train. The thick bastard couldn't even do that properly. He missed the train.

OSCAR. That's not true, Granddad. He's the strongest man in Manchester.

*Beat.*

JOHN. They never loved you. How could they? They didn't know how to do it.

OSCAR. That's not true, Granddad. They always loved each other and they always loved me.

JOHN. You're making yourself look incredibly ridiculous.

*Beat.*

When they left you on our doorstep that Christmas you didn't even have your own underpants. You were wearing a pair of your mum's old knickers. They were so full of dried piss they were stiff. They were stuck to your skin. We had to put you in the bath and peel them off you. You screamed the house down. You must have been wearing them for days. They were probably like that when they put them on you.

*Beat.*

That's how much they loved you.

*Beat.*

Why have you never seen your mum? Why has she never sent you a birthday card or called to see if you're okay? Why did she abandon you with nothing but a dead dog for company?

OSCAR. Because sometimes we do things that we don't really mean and then find it very hard to say we are wrong. It's why you still pretend that you love Nana.

JOHN. I do love your nana.

OSCAR. I don't think you do.

I don't think you can have ever loved anyone in your life, Granddad.

JOHN. I've never loved you, Oscar. No one has. No one ever will.

OSCAR. You don't have the honesty needed to love.

JOHN *goes over to the bird stand.*

JOHN *looks at it.*

JOHN *looks at* OSCAR.

JOHN *picks up the hammer.*

JOHN *starts to smash it up systematically. He is quite controlled at first but as the deconstruction escalates he is almost singing in his ferocity. It is as though he isn't smashing the bird stand but something bigger, maybe himself.*

My dad's brain doesn't work that well any more. It's stuck in another time. He thinks he is the same age as me. He might not have worked on the tallest crane in the world or be the bravest man in Manchester but the blinding blizzards in his head aren't controlled by the same fear that blind the truth in yours, Granddad.

*Pause.*

I love you.

JOHN *leaves.*

OSCAR *is alone.*

## Scene Seven

*Two years later. Autumn. A small wall by a canal. A broken street lamp.*

*Late evening sunshine casts giant shadows.*

*Three people sit on the wall.*

JEAN (*sixty-four*) *is sat at one end of the wall.*

*Her handbag is on her knee.*

HELEN (*twenty-six*) *is sat on the other end of the wall.*

OSCAR (*twelve*) *is sat in the middle of the wall.*

*He is wearing a school uniform. The jumper is pulled up over his head so the shape of his face is stretched through the jumper.*

*All three are eating ice creams in silence.*

OSCAR *is trying to eat his through his jumper.*

HELEN. I watched an old man die this morning. On a disused railway footbridge. I watched his lips turn from red to blue.

He had no shoes and socks on. Have you ever watched someone die? Has he? I bet you haven't. I bet you three pounds seventy-eight, a battery, and a peanut which is all I've got in my pocket that you haven't. Are you not going to talk to me?

JEAN. You can't eat your ice cream through your jumper. It's impossible. You're just making a mess.

HELEN. I've been eating grapefruit a lot recently. Grapefruit. It's bloody lovely. Have you ever tried it?

JEAN. He doesn't eat fresh fruit do you, Oscar?

OSCAR *doesn't answer.*

He doesn't. It goes right through him. Comes out like a flock of sparrows.

HELEN. If you eat it it's so refreshing. Pink grapefruit. I've got these white grapefruit now. I bought ten of them so I can have one every day. Five white ones and five pink ones. The pink ones are expensive but the white ones aren't. I don't know why. Must be harder to grow or something. Anyway this man. This old dying man. He was nearly naked. I could see his erect dick peeping through his green dressing gown. Just before he died he asked me to show him my right breast. It was very cold and frosty but I did. He asked to smell my hair. I let him. I touched his hand and he died very, very quickly.

*Beat.*

When you talk to him does he answer you straight away? He's quite…

JEAN. He can talk. He's very capable. When he wants.

HELEN. I've brought him a biscuit. A chocolate one. I went out especially to get it. It's a treat.

HELEN *takes a chocolate biscuit from her coat pocket and holds it out.*

*She talks to him as though he were deaf.*

Do you want this chocolate biscuit?

OSCAR *stands with his jumper still over his head and goes over to* JEAN.

OSCAR *whispers in* JEAN*'s ear.*

JEAN. Yes you can. Don't wind him up though.

OSCAR *runs off.*

JEAN *and* HELEN *watch him go.*

*They slowly eat their ice creams.*

He's gone to speak to the ice-cream man. He knows him very well. He visits our road every evening without fail. Mr Stone is a very nice man. Always smokes a cigar as he serves you. Doesn't charge for crushed nuts if you give him a wink. He's very well-to-do. Got a sunbed in his loft I believe. He's very fond of Oscar. They had a fall-out over the summer though. Oscar squirted the hosepipe through his van window. Most of his ice cream melted. Our road's the start of his round so you can imagine what trouble it caused. A local outcry. He smashed Oscar's head against his counter. Gave him a deep cut on his eyebrow. Bled for hours. I would've gone mad, kicked up a bit of a fuss but he deserved everything he got. Turned out he'd had it coming for a long time. He'd started an ice-cream feud between Mr Stone and another ice-cream man. An Algerian called Black Bruno. Oscar had been going from one to the other telling each the other one had been questioning the quality of their ice cream. That's like a red rag to a bull for an ice-cream man. They ended up fighting in a park full of children one Saturday afternoon. The kids went mad. Showered them with spit. It made the evening paper.

HELEN. I'll leave his biscuit on the wall for him. He might want it when he comes back. I could never resist a chocolate biscuit when I was his age.

HELEN *stands and places the chocolate biscuit on the wall where* OSCAR *has been sitting.*

*She returns to her end of the wall and sits.*

*They both continue to eat their ice creams.*

*Silence.*

You look different.

JEAN. Yes.

*Pause.*

HELEN. Not how I remember.

JEAN. No.

*Pause.*

HELEN. You don't know what to say do you?

JEAN. No I don't. You don't make it easy. You really don't. You never have.

HELEN. Words. Difficult sometimes. Aren't they.

*Silence.*

JEAN. I thought you might have died.

HELEN. No.

HELEN *puts her ice cream on the floor and stamps on it.*

I hate ice cream. Tastes like dirty cocks.

HELEN *sits on the wall.*

*She rubs one of her eyes.*

*She yawns.*

*She hums loudly.*

JEAN. That's what I thought. I've had visions of you dying in so many different ways. A different picture in my head every day. I didn't want them there. Not when they first came. They just scratched through my eyeballs when I wasn't looking. Like beautiful stained-glass windows shining in my brain. I started keeping a diary. To write them down. They were important. A diary of how my daughter died. I've got seven of them now. All in different colours. I keep them in my handbag.

JEAN *gets the diaries out of her handbag and opens one at random dates.*

Tuesday eighth February –

In a dirty toilet gagged on her own sick.

Friday thirteenth May –

Strangled in a muddy field underneath a broken scarecrow.

I kept on thinking I'd see you on the news at teatime or something. Hear about you on a car radio through a wound-down window at some traffic lights. Never alive. Always dead. Always totally destroyed.

HELEN. How is he? How is my son?

JEAN. He's not your son. He stopped being your son the night you dumped him on our doorstep. The same night you stopped being my daughter. He'll never be your son.

*Pause.*

HELEN. How is he?

JEAN. You can't say his name can you? Your mouth can't shape the word.

*Beat.*

HELEN. How is... he?

*Beat.*

JEAN. Oscar. He needs to be loved. People find his shyness very vulgar. It takes a lot of guts to be gentle and kind.

HELEN. Right.

*Beat.*

Dad. He alright?

JEAN. He still puts his coat on, zips it up and goes out looking for you. Gets on a bus. Goes wherever it takes him. I tell him not to bother. He thought he found you once. Rotting away

in a falling-down factory. Dead on a shit-stained mattress.
Surrounded by milk bottles full of piss and dried up
condoms. It nearly killed him. It wasn't you but that didn't
matter. It might as well have been. If you cut a hope in half is
the bit that's left really worth it.

HELEN *laughs. She stops herself.*

HELEN. I've been all over the place. I think I walked to
Scotland once. I don't know how I did it. I don't know which
way I went. The roads I walked down. I can't remember. I
just arrived in places. Existed for a bit. Not living. Just
ticking over. Everywhere I went was just black.

JEAN. Oscar doesn't see his...

HELEN. His dad?

JEAN. He doesn't see him any more. I don't let him. He's not
really a person any more. He's just a shell. I go and see him
quite a bit on my own. Just sit in an orange plastic chair.
Watch him dribble into a child's bib they put on him. I watch
him struggle to control his bowels. His muck squirts up his
back. I watch him tug at the catheter that drains his bladder. I
feed him biscuits until he's sick and biting chunks out of his
own tongue. It makes me smile. Sometimes a little bit of wee
comes out. I know it's wrong but it makes me feel all warm
inside. I think we all get punished for the bad things we do.

HELEN (*simultaneous*). I'm pregnant.

JEAN (*simultaneous*). I'm dying.

I am. I'm dying. I'm going to be dead very soon. No one
knows. Not even your dad. Not even Oscar. I don't even
know why I told you because you don't mean anything to
me. You're a stranger. It just feels the most important thing
in the world that in this tiny moment I tell you I'm going to
die. That it hurts. That I'm scared. That I'm very tired.
You've got raspberry sauce all over your face.

JEAN *spits on a tissue and wipes* HELEN's *face clean.*

I've brought you a cigarette.

JEAN *gets a cigarette out of her handbag.*

You do still smoke don't you?

HELEN. When I can.

JEAN. I got it off a teenager. I offered him some money. He wouldn't take it.

HELEN *takes the cigarettes from* JEAN.

*She strikes a match on the wall.*

*She lights a cigarette and her face is brightened by the flame.*

*She lets the whole match burn.*

*She throws it in the canal.*

*She smokes the cigarette.*

*She rubs her stomach.*

*The street lamp starts to buzz and flicker. It casts intermittent orange light over the canal and falls on the shape of* OSCAR *standing underneath.*

*He is silent and still.*

*He watches* HELEN *and* JEAN.

*They don't see him.*

HELEN. I sent him a birthday card. It had a badge on it.

JEAN. Yes.

HELEN. Did he like it?

JEAN. I didn't give it to him.

HELEN. I understand.

JEAN. No you don't.

HELEN. Tried to phone.

JEAN. Changed the number.

HELEN. I know. Ex-directory. Gone all posh.

JEAN. Had to.

HELEN. Why?

JEAN. Nuisance calls. All the time. Day and night.

HELEN. Did you?

JEAN. I knew it was you. I know how you breathe. I've
watched you sleep remember.

HELEN. I only wanted to hear him speak. One small word. I
was curious.

*Pause.*

Sorry to hear about you dying and everything. What is it?
Cancer or sommat. It's funny.

HELEN *laughs.*

It's not. Sorry for laughing. It's a nervous thing. It's cos I'm
shocked. It's not quite sunk in. I love you.

JEAN. Do you?

HELEN. Mmmm.

JEAN. I don't feel loved.

HELEN. Don't you?

JEAN. No I don't.

HELEN. Can I have some money?

JEAN. I haven't got any.

HELEN. Give us some money.

JEAN. I've told you.

HELEN. You're lying.

JEAN. I'm not.

HELEN. You are.

*Beat.*

I watched you draw his benefit this morning at the Post Office. I followed you. I hid behind the postcard rack. I pretended to be a foreigner. I saw you put it in your purse. Twenty pounds forty. Two weeks' worth. Two ten-pound notes and two twenty-pence pieces. Am I right? You gave him one twenty pence to get a penny mix. That leaves twenty pounds twenty minus the ice creams you bought. I'm not stupid. Do you think I'm stupid? I'm not stupid. I was always very good at maths.

HELEN *grabs hold of* JEAN's *handbag.*

*They struggle.*

Give me your fucking bag you skinny fucking tramp.

HELEN *rips the handbag from* JEAN.

*She turns it upside down and empties its contents on the floor.*

*She scratches around the dirt.*

*She finds the purse and takes the ten-pound note out.*

What's wrong with your face?

JEAN. He needs new underpants. His old ones are all baggy. His balls keep falling out when he does PE. His teachers complained. He's getting teased. I need to buy him some. That's what that's for.

HELEN *throws the purse on the floor.*

HELEN. Who do you think you're talking to, you?

HELEN *blows on the end of the cigarette and it glows red hot.*

*She threatens* JEAN *with it.*

He grew inside me. Deep down in the arse of your barren stomach you know it's true. That fucking hurts you doesn't it? It fucking burns your insides out like drain cleaner. I can feel the panic from here. I can warm my hands on it. Nothing

good ever came from your cunt. Only me. What a crying
shame that is. Mother. You're just a dying pig waiting for the
soil to fall over your head.

*The street lamp settles.*

*They both become aware of* OSCAR*'s presence.*

HELEN *hardens. She doesn't look at him.*

*Tears fall from* JEAN*'s eyes.*

OSCAR. Granddad's been having a lot of problems with his
bottom recently. He had this lump on his right bumcheek. He
said it hurt like hell. He went to the doctor but she said it was
just an in-growing hair so he left it, but it turned into a pus-
filled blister and when he sat down yesterday to eat his
boiled potatoes and bacon he forgot to sit on his cushion. It
must have burst because it seeped through his pants on to the
seat. He said it didn't hurt but it did smell a lot.

OSCAR *goes to the biscuit on the wall.*

*He unwraps it and puts the wrapper in his pocket.*

*He puts the whole biscuit in his mouth and chews it.*

*He goes to* HELEN *and spits the chewed-up biscuit in her
face.*

HELEN *is still.*

You could have come back just once. Looked through my
window while I was asleep. Watched me play in the school
playground through the wire fence. Followed me when I was
going to the shops for Nana on my bike. Watched what
sweets I bought. Seen me crying when I fell over. Kissed me
better. Looked at the first picture I'd painted. Polished my
shoes. Made me a birthday cake. Looked after me when I
was poorly. Slept on my bed. Holding me in your arms. I
might have missed you more then.

*Beat.*

It's good to be silent sometimes. Close everything down.

*Beat.*

My name is Oscar. I am twelve. I like animals especially
birds. I have size five shoes. I don't like wearing wool
because it makes me wheeze. I've never eaten chips. I like
watching television but prefer listening to the radio. I support
the greatest football team in the world. Manchester United. I
hate City. They are scum. I was circumcised by Dr Singh
four months, two weeks and five days ago. I still have the
disposable stitches from my willy in a clear hospital sample
jar. I sometimes put them in my mouth at night. I once had
the runs when I was playing out and had to do a poo in a red
telephone box. I wiped my bum on a cigarette box. I have
also wee'd against a lamp post nine doors away from my
house just for fun of it. I've never been in love with a girl. I
don't think. I've never even kissed one. I don't think. I never
used to like chocolate but I do now. I like Mars Bars the best
but only when they are soft. If they are hard or have been in
the fridge I put them in my pants to warm them up. I like
salt-and-vinegar crisps with extra salt. I love Coca-Cola. I
don't have many friends. I don't have any friends. But I
don't mind. I know I am a good person. I think I've always
told the truth. I don't walk on cracks in the ground. I always
salute magpies. I'm very lucky. I think you gave birth to me.
That's my history. Who I am. My place in it.

OSCAR *wets himself.*

*A puddle forms at his feet.*

I didn't think it would be like this. I didn't think I would
have to be the one making all the effort.

*Beat.*

We are all silly aren't we? The silences we can fall in to.
Like giant holes in the snow. It must get harder when you're
older. When you're an adult. The responsibility to keep the
silences away must be deafening. I decide on my quietness.
When to use it. When it will achieve the loudest bang. The
biggest explosion. Like now.

*Silence.*

OSCAR *falls silent. Everything stops. Nothing.*

I stopped the world. I stopped it spinning. Did you feel it? The stillness. The noise.

HELEN *covers her face.*

Why do you have to hide all the time? Cover your face like that? You should look at me.

*Beat.*

Let me know that you want to see me.

HELEN *looks small.*

That's what I used to do when I was young. Try and make myself too small to see.

HELEN. You are young.

OSCAR. I'm not. I've been old for ages me. What do you want?

*Beat.*

I can remember the day I started to speak. I remember the hour and the minute. I remember the colour of everything. Can you, Nana?

JEAN *nods.*

(*To* HELEN.) Can you?

HELEN *is still.*

I don't know you. Not really. But I can see it. There is something good about you.

*Pause.*

HELEN. I love you.

OSCAR. You shouldn't. You will only be disappointed. It's a sacrifice. Don't you think. Mum.

Why are you crying?

HELEN. I don't know.

Goodbye, Oscar.

*This is goodbye for ever. They will never see each other again. They stand looking at each other.*

OSCAR. Goodbye.

HELEN *leaves*.

JEAN *watches her leave*.

JEAN *takes an Extra Strong Mint from her bag and eats it*.

JEAN *offers* OSCAR *a mint and he accepts it. He sits on the wall and eats the mint.*

### Scene Eight

*A few months later. January. The bathroom at* JEAN *and* JOHN*'s house.*

*An old white enamel bath.*

*The taps are running and eventually the water will overflow.*

*The water steams.*

*A black suit, white shirt and a black tie hang on a hook. A pair of black shoes and socks sit underneath them on the floor.*

JEAN (*sixty-five*) *sits on a wooden chair.*

*She sees the bath overflowing and turns off the taps.*

OSCAR (*thirteen*) *emerges from underneath the water.*

OSCAR. How long, Nana?

*Beat.*

Nana?

*Beat.*

Nana, how long?

JEAN *doesn't answer.*

OSCAR *takes another deep breath and disappears underneath the water.*

*After some time,* OSCAR *emerges again, releasing his held breath.*

How long, Nana?

JEAN. About half a minute.

*Pause.*

OSCAR (*looking at his hands*). My fingers are all wrinkly. Old man's hands.

JEAN. If you stay in there much longer you'll turn into an old man.

*Beat.*

OSCAR. Nana?

I keep dreaming the world is ending.

JEAN. It's just a dream.

OSCAR. When will it?

JEAN. What?

OSCAR. End.

JEAN. The world?

OSCAR. Yes.

JEAN. When it's ready.

JEAN *goes to the bath.*

OSCAR *gives her a bar of soap.*

JEAN *rubs the bar of soap onto* OSCAR's *head and works up a lather.*

JEAN *washes his hair in silence.*

OSCAR. Do you want to know my dream, Nana?

That soldiers came.

they dragged people onto the road

the women by the hair

they castrated the men and made them eat it

shot them through the face.

Locked all the children in a garage

poured petrol through the roof

set it on fire.

Pissed into the flames.

I saw the body of a baby

I think he was my son.

Dogs eating his body.

Told the women to bury their dead under the concrete road.

It took days.

They buried the men on a Saturday morning.

I was in the grave.

Broken. Twisted. Bodies.

I lay among them.

Quiet.

I was pulled out alive.

The soldier said he would kill me tomorrow

I begged him to kill me today.

I begged him to shoot me.

He gave me clothes and water.

They made me watch them kill.

They had sex with dead people.

Animals.

I saw an old woman who looked like you.

Naked.

I waved.

She was walking over the dead.

The soldiers threw bricks at her face.

They burnt her with cigarettes.

They whipped her with sticks.

They made her sing nursery rhymes

as they cut off her breasts

with garden shears.

They ripped her apart and hung her from a street lamp.

One leg one side of the road.

One leg on the other side of the road.

The soldiers left in the morning.

I dreamt that.

That everyone I know dies.

That I'm left alone. Everywhere is empty. No sound.
Nothing.

Just me on a road of dead bodies.

When will I be like everybody else?

JEAN *doesn't answer. She is looking up at the sky.*

What's up there?

JEAN *still doesn't answer.*

OSCAR *disappears under the water again.*

*After some time he emerges.*

When do you think my willy will grow, Nana?

*Beat.*

Do you think I will wake up one morning and it will have grown massive? Or do you think that it will stay the same and my body will just get big? I don't know what would be better. The biggest willy I've ever seen was on a donkey. It was weeing on the sand. Making puddles. If my willy grows that big I haven't got a pair of underpants or trousers to put it in. I'd have to walk around with nothing on. I don't think I'd like that. It might get a bit embarrassing. Especially on the bus or in maths when I have to collect the books in. That's when my willy always gets hard for no reason. I don't know why.

JEAN *gets a large white bath towel and holds it open.*

Everyone talks about willies in my school. I don't see what the fuss is all about.

OSCAR *indicates with his finger for her to turn around so she can't see his naked body.*

JEAN *gives the towel to OSCAR and turns around.*

OSCAR *gets out of the bath and wraps the towel around his wet body.*

There's a group of boys who show each other theirs. They do it in the toilets at breaktime and dinner. There's six of them. They stand in a cubicle and measure whose is bigger with the straight edge on a protractor. I think they take it very seriously because there's always one of them taking notes. I don't know what about. He might trace the outline of each willy on the pages of his book. Just to keep track of any changes. They all concentrate very hard when they are doing it. Their faces look like this.

JEAN *turns back and begins to dry OSCAR with towel.*

There's a tall one with ginger spiky hair and a leg brace called Frogger. He's a prefect. He asked me if I wanted to measure his once. He even offered me the use of his protractor. He said it was brand new. That no one else had ever used it. He was very softly spoken and polite. I felt I'd let him down when I told him thank you but no thank you. I thought he was going to cry. He punched me in the face instead.

JEAN *gets* OSCAR*'s white underpants and he steps into them.*

OSCAR *pulls them up.*

I never go to the toilet at school any more. They're always dirty anyway. Bits of poo and wee and soggy toilet paper everywhere. Even on the ceiling. No one knows how to use the toilet properly at my school.

JEAN *gets* OSCAR*'s white shirt.*

OSCAR *puts his arms into the sleeves and she does the buttons up.*

No I hope my willy doesn't get too big. I wouldn't want it getting in the way.

JEAN *gets* OSCAR*'s black trousers and he steps into them.*

OSCAR *pulls them up. He tucks his shirt in and fastens his trousers.*

Granddad's got a big willy hasn't he, Nana? I've seen it. He was playing with it in front of the mirror. The one on his wardrobe door. He was naked. He didn't have a protractor. He didn't see me watching him. He was crying.

JEAN *gives* OSCAR *the black tie.*

OSCAR *tries to tie it but can't.*

JEAN *ties the tie.*

He wiped the mirror clean with his handkerchief. That's when he saw me. He told me to fuck off and closed the door.

JEAN. I know.

OSCAR. I nearly told him to fuck off back.

JEAN. I know.

OSCAR. I didn't.

JEAN. I know.

JEAN *gets* OSCAR's *socks from the shoes. She puts them on him.*

OSCAR. I like it when it's just me and you, Nana.

JEAN. I do too.

OSCAR. Granddad can't interrupt us.

*Beat.*

He's ignoring you.

JEAN. He isn't ignoring me, Oscar. He's just sad at the moment.

OSCAR. I thought he was going to hit me.

JEAN. He didn't.

JEAN *gets* OSCAR's *shoes. She sets them down and he steps into them. She ties the laces.*

OSCAR. Nana, you look beautiful.

JEAN. Thank you, Oscar.

JEAN *gets the black suit jacket.*

OSCAR *puts his arm through the sleeves and* JEAN *eases it on.*

JEAN *combs* OSCAR's *hair neatly.*

You won't be here soon will you? Why does everyone leave me, Nana? I'm sorry if I did anything wrong.

JEAN *goes out.*

I…

OSCAR *is left alone.*

## Scene Nine

*A year later. July. The hottest day of the year.* JEAN *and* JOHN's *back garden.*

*The sun burns.*

*An old bath stands in the garden acting as an improvised water feature and rainwater butt.*

*A home-made swing hangs somewhere.*

JOHN (*sixty-seven*) *is digging a hole.*

*As he digs he empties the soil on the ground.*

*By the side of him there is a watering can and a rose bush still in its plastic pot.*

*Nearby on a small wooden table there is a jug of water and an empty glass.*

*After some time he stops digging.*

*He pours a glass of water and downs it in one.*

*He goes to the bath tub.*

*He takes his shoes off. He takes his socks off and puts them in his shoes.*

*He rolls his trouser legs up and steps into the paddling pool.*

*He paddles.*

*He takes out a handkerchief from his trouser pocket and soaks it in the water.*

*He wrings it out and drapes it over his head.*

*He closes his eyes.*

*He is still.*

OSCAR (*fourteen*) *enters.*

*He is carrying a goldfish in a clear plastic bag full of water. He holds it out in front of him and examines it.*

*He quietly creeps up to the paddling pool and splashes water all over* JOHN.

JOHN (*shocked, angry, and incoherent*). Absolutely bloody stupid you are.

OSCAR *holds the goldfish out in front of him.*

Bloody stupid.

*Beat.*

What's that?

OSCAR. I won it. It's a goldfish. I won it at the fair. I won it for you. I thought you'd like it.

JOHN. I'm soaking wet now.

OSCAR. I won it on one of them stalls where you have to hook a rubber duck on to the end of a pole. It took me ages. I did it though. I won. I won it for you.

*Beat.*

JOHN. You shouldn't have wasted your money. We haven't even got a fish tank. Where you going to keep a fish if you haven't even got a fish tank?

*Beat.*

Eh? Where you going to keep it?

*Beat.*

Bloody thick sometimes you.

*Beat.*

Giving your money to Gyppos.

*Beat.*

It'll be dead in a day.

JOHN *gets out of the bath tub and leaves.*

OSCAR *takes his shoes off.*

OSCAR *takes his socks off and puts them in his shoes.*

OSCAR *rolls his jeans up and stands in the paddling pool.*

OSCAR *opens the bag and empties the fish in to the bath tub.*

OSCAR *watches it swim around his feet.*

JOHN *enters with a towel.*

*He stops and looks at* OSCAR.

JOHN *sits on the ground and dries his feet with the towel and then puts his socks on.*

JOHN *puts his shoes on and ties the laces.*

JOHN *rolls his trouser legs down.*

JOHN *continues digging.*

OSCAR *looks at* JOHN.

OSCAR *gets out of the bath tub and leaves.*

JOHN *pulls a makeshift cross out of the ground that he had erected years before for the grave of* OSCAR's *dog and puts it on the ground.*

JOHN *goes to the goldfish in the bath tub and watches it swim.*

JOHN *spits in the paddling pool.*

JOHN *goes back to his spade and digs.*

OSCAR *returns carrying a massive stuffed toy. It dwarfs him.*

OSCAR. Granddad.

JOHN *doesn't answer.*

Granddad.

JOHN *doesn't answer.*

Granddad.

JOHN *doesn't answer.*

I won this for you too.

JOHN *turns to* OSCAR.

I thought it would make you happy.

JOHN. Where did you get that?

OSCAR. The fair.

JOHN. No you didn't.

OSCAR. I did.

JOHN. I don't believe you.

OSCAR. I did.

JOHN. Where did you pinch it from?

OSCAR. I didn't.

JOHN. Pinch it from some children's home or something?

OSCAR. No.

JOHN. Where did you get it?

OSCAR. I won it. I won it for you, Granddad. I didn't rob it. I won it for you.

*Pause.*

JOHN. What do I want a teddy bear for? What am I going to do with that? Just mess up the house. Get in the way. Covered in dust.

*Beat.*

You want to start thinking about growing up a bit. Playing with teddy bears. Very childish, Oscar. You want to start thinking about changing a bit. Being more responsible. Being more mature.

*Beat.*

Do you hear me?

*Beat.*

Do you hear me?

*Beat.*

I won't ask you again. Do you hear me?

OSCAR. Yes.

OSCAR *sits the teddy bear on the swing and pushes it.*

JOHN *stops digging and pulls out a black-plastic bin bag that is worn and covered in soil. Inside the bag are the remains of* OSCAR*'s dog.*

JOHN *throws it on the ground.*

JOHN. Bag of bones now. Nothing left.

OSCAR *stops pushing the teddy bear and looks at* JOHN.

OSCAR. You shouldn't dig up dead things, Granddad. Should just let things be.

JOHN. Who says?

OSCAR. That's what Nana would say. Just let things be.

JOHN *laughs to himself.*

JOHN. Remember the night we buried him?

OSCAR. No.

JOHN. It was three days before Christmas.

OSCAR. I don't remember.

JOHN. You were four.

OSCAR. I don't remember.

JOHN. The night your mum left you.

OSCAR. No, Granddad. I don't remember.

OSCAR *goes to the swing and sits on it.*

JOHN. The ground was frozen solid. All cracked and broken. I
should've just thrown him in the canal. Made a hole in the
ice and dropped him in. I should have. I didn't. I didn't
because I promised your mum.

*Beat.*

It took me an hour to dig a hole that night.

*Beat.*

I'm going to plant a rose bush here. Scatter your nana's
ashes. It was always her favourite place in the garden. God
knows why. Contaminated if you ask me.

OSCAR *pushes the teddy bear on the swing.*

JOHN *turns the rose upside down and takes it out of its
plastic pot.*

OSCAR. Why don't you like me?

JOHN *loosens its roots and puts it in the hole in the ground.*

Why don't you like me, Granddad?

JOHN *fills the soil that he has dug out back into the hole and
firms the soil around the rose with his foot.*

Why don't you like me?

JOHN *gets the watering can and waters the rose.*

JOHN *leaves.*

OSCAR *stops pushing the teddy bear and goes over to the
wheel barrow.*

*He looks at the dead dog.*

*He rips open the black bag and touches the remains of the
dog.*

*He goes to the paddling pool and washes his hands in the
water.*

JOHN *returns with an urn containing the ashes of his dead wife*.

OSCAR *holds his hands out*.

Can I hold the ashes?

JOHN *goes to the rose bush and kneels*.

I think I should hold them, Granddad.

JOHN *takes the lid off the urn*.

Give me the ashes.

JOHN. What?

OSCAR. Give me the ashes.

JOHN. Wha... What?

OSCAR *goes to* JOHN.

OSCAR (*playfully kicking* JOHN *softly*). Give me the ashes.

JOHN. Stop it –

OSCAR (*playfully kicking* JOHN *a bit harder*). Give me the ashes.

JOHN. Don't –

OSCAR (*playfully kicking* JOHN). Give me the ashes.

JOHN. Will you –

OSCAR (*kicking* JOHN). Give me the ashes.

JOHN. I told –

OSCAR (*kicking* JOHN *harder*). Give me the ashes.

JOHN. I want –

OSCAR (*kicking* JOHN *hard*). Give me the ashes.

JOHN *gives* OSCAR *the ashes*.

OSCAR *goes to the paddling pool and stands in it*.

JOHN. I do like you.

OSCAR. No you don't.

*Beat.*

I know you don't. If you did you wouldn't always hurt me.

JOHN. I do like you.

OSCAR. I don't mind that you don't like me. Just because I'm your daughter's son doesn't mean that you have to like me. It isn't the law. I don't think you can get sent to prison for not liking me.

OSCAR *puts his hand in the urn and takes out a handful of ashes. They run through his fingers.*

There was this girl in my class called Lisa Felix. I really didn't like her. She really didn't like me. There was something chemical about the way we hated each other.

She got leukaemia. She wasn't in school for ages. Then one day she came back. Mrs Troth my teacher told us that she was going to die. That she was coming back to say goodbye to everyone. We all made cards for her. On the inside of my card I wrote:

To Lisa,

I will always hate you. I don't care that you are dying because I hate you. Just because you have cancer doesn't change the fact that you're a cunt. You were before you had cancer. You still will be after you're dead.

Good luck,

Oscar.

JOHN. You cruel b–

OSCAR. I gave her the card and she read it. She looked at me and started to laugh. She laughed so much that the tube up her nose made it bleed. It dripped over her lips onto her chin and she licked it with her tongue. I was honest with her and she appreciated that. It didn't matter that we didn't like each other because we both accepted that was just the way it was. I never saw Lisa again.

I don't care that you don't like me, Granddad, but I'd like to know why you don't. Is it something I've done or is it just something chemical?

OSCAR *goes to empty the ashes.*

JOHN. Give me the ashes.

OSCAR. No.

JOHN. Give me the ashes.

OSCAR. Tell me why you hate me.

*Almost emptying the ashes out.*

JOHN. I don't…

JOHN *snatches the ashes from* OSCAR.

I don't like…

JOHN *takes a spoonful of the ashes and holds it to his mouth.*

…like you, Oscar. I really don't like you. I've tried to like you for years but I just can't. I hate myself for hating you and then I hate you more for making me hate myself. I look at you and I feel sick. My stomach feels sick. You make my whole body feel sick.

JOHN *puts the ashes in his mouth. He drinks some water from the glass. He battles to swallow the ashes.*

I hate you because my daughter went.

JOHN *takes another spoonful, eats, drinks and swallows.*

I hate you because she never came back.

JOHN *takes another spoonful, eats, drinks and swallows.*

I hate you because you remind me of everything lost.

JOHN *takes another spoonful, eats, drinks and swallows.*

I hate you because I haven't made your life better.

JOHN *puts the empty urn on the floor.*

OSCAR. I love you, Granddad.

JOHN *walks off.*

OSCAR *sits on the swing.*

*He swings.*

**Scene Ten**

*A year later. Bonfire Night. Anywhere in Manchester.*

*Darkness.*

*Fireworks and revelry can be heard in the distance. The sound is ambiguous. It could be mistaken for a city in a state of panic or unrest. The fireworks could be gunshots and mortar explosions. The shouts and cheers could be something more sinister.*

OSCAR *(fifteen) sits alone.*

*A torch is by his side.*

*A GIRL (fifteen) enters.*

*Her lips and mouth are bloodied.*

*Her clothes are ripped.*

*She doesn't notice OSCAR.*

OSCAR *sees her and shines the torch in her face.*

*The GIRL is still.*

OSCAR *throws a stone at the GIRL.*

*The* GIRL *is still.*

OSCAR *takes a can out of his backpack.*

OSCAR *opens his can.*

OSCAR *offers the can to the* GIRL.

*The* GIRL *is still.*

OSCAR *walks halfway towards the* GIRL *and places the can on the ground.*

OSCAR *takes off his coat and offers it to the* GIRL.

*The* GIRL *looks at* OSCAR.

*The* GIRL *takes the coat.*

*They look at each other.*

*A firework explodes overhead and the moment freezes in time.*

OSCAR. You should put it on. It's freezing. I don't feel the cold.

  *The* GIRL *puts the coat on.*

  OSCAR *goes to the can and takes a mouthful.*

  OSCAR *looks away.*

  OSCAR *goes to his backpack and takes out two sparklers.*

  *He goes halfway towards the* GIRL.

  Do you want a sparkler?

  *The* GIRL *looks at* OSCAR.

  *The* GIRL *takes one of the sparklers.*

  OSCAR *lights the* GIRL's *sparkler and then his own.*

  *They both hold their sparklers in the darkness.*

  *Their sparklers stop sparkling.*

  OSCAR *takes both of the sparklers and pours some of the drink from the can on them.*

*The sparklers hiss and smoke.*

OSCAR *and the* GIRL *are apart.*

OSCAR *looks away.*

Who's done that?

*Pause.*

Who hurt you?

*The* GIRL *opens her hand to reveal a flower head. She has been holding it for a long time.*

*It is crushed but it still resembles what it was.*

GIRL. She spat in my mouth.

They laughed.

I swallowed it.

I opened my mouth.

They all spat in it.

I swallowed it all.

I wasn't sick.

I didn't scream.

They held me down.

She tore my tights.

I didn't cry.

I wet my knickers.

It went on her shoe.

She wiped it on my face.

She shoved a beer bottle up me.

She pissed on my face.

They took my mum's flowers.

It was white but now it's red.

*OSCAR goes to his backpack.*

*He takes out a bottle of water.*

*He goes to the GIRL.*

*He holds his hand out.*

*The GIRL gives him the stained flower.*

*OSCAR opens the bottle of water and pours it over the flower.*

*OSCAR rubs the flower petals gently.*

*The blood staining the flower runs and washes off returning the flower to its original white colour.*

*OSCAR gives the flower back to the GIRL.*

Thank you.

*The GIRL stands and goes to leave.*

OSCAR. Are you going?

GIRL. Yes. I think so.

*Beat.*

Are you?

OSCAR. No, I'm staying here.

GIRL. On your own?

OSCAR. Yes.

*The GIRL goes to take OSCAR's coat off and give it him back.*

You can keep my coat.

GIRL. Thank you.

*Beat.*

Goodbye.

OSCAR. Yes. Goodbye.

*The* GIRL *leaves* OSCAR *alone.*

*Silence.*

*The* GIRL *returns.*

*They stand looking each other.*

*The* GIRL *holds out her hand and offers the flower.*

OSCAR *looks away.*

GIRL. Do you want this?

*Beat.*

Do you?

OSCAR *takes the flower.*

*He looks at it.*

*He looks at the* GIRL.

*He picks at the petals.*

*He is controlled at first but the intensity of the destruction escalates.*

*He destroys it. It's as though he's ruining something bigger. Maybe himself.*

You're not a bad person.

*Beat.*

You're absolutely not by the way.

*Beat.*

OSCAR. Neither are you.

*Beat.*

GIRL. Are you crying?

OSCAR. A little bit.

GIRL. Can I have a sip of your can?

*OSCAR picks up the can.*

*He wipes it and gives it to the GIRL.*

*The GIRL drinks from the can.*

*She wipes it and passes it to OSCAR.*

*OSCAR drinks from the can.*

Can I have some chocolate?

*OSCAR smiles.*

*He goes to the backpack and returns with it.*

*He turns the bag upside down and loads of different chocolate bars tumble out.*

OSCAR. I like chocolate.

*The GIRL sifts through the chocolate.*

*As she does, OSCAR pulls a Mars Bar out from the seat of his pants.*

*The GIRL looks at him.*

(*Embarrassed.*) I have to melt Mars Bars a bit. I can't eat them hard. They have to be a bit soft.

*The GIRL picks up a chocolate bar and starts to eat it.*

It's my birthday.

*Beat.*

GIRL. Happy birthday.

*The GIRL looks at OSCAR.*

Can I hold your hand?

*OSCAR looks at the GIRL.*

OSCAR. I don't know how.

*Beat.*

I don't.

*Beat.*

No one ever has.

GIRL. I will.

OSCAR. You don't have to.

*The GIRL holds her hand out.*

*Beat.*

GIRL. Hello.

*Beat.*

OSCAR. Yes.

*OSCAR holds his hand out.*

Hello.

*They hold hands slowly. They look at each other.*

*Silence.*

GIRL. Will everything just go dark?

*Beat.*

Will it just be a moment?

OSCAR. I think it will be nothing. I think it will be alright.

*The ground starts to crack and fracture.*

*It begins to rain heavily.*

*They sit in the rain.*

*OSCAR closes his eyes.*

*The world begins to darken and its presence falls away.*

*They are the centre of the universe surrounded by stars dancing in the darkness.*

*The End.*

## ANDREW SHERIDAN

Andrew trained as an actor at Rose Bruford College and has performed extensively in award-winning theatre, TV and film.

Andrew's debut play *Winterlong* was the joint winner of the 2008 Bruntwood Playwriting Competition.